Welsh
Salad Days

Welsh Salad Days

Food and drink from Wales to the End of the World

by Dave Frost

with recipes by Barbara Rottner Frost

CONTENTS

LIST OF ILLUSTRATIONS

PREFACE

We started to write this book when we were asked for recipes for the salads we prepared in our shop, an organic food shop that we ran in Aberystwyth from 1987 to 1993. When we came to write down the recipes we found we needed to explain why we used particular ingredients, and the importance of fresh herbs, fruit and dressings. Doing so meant setting out many of our basic ideas about food and diet, and to elaborate them further involved the inclusion of other recipes and other influences, so the book became more than just salads. The recipes that Barbara created for the shop are listed in the final chapter along with many others that we've brought together from our travels from Wales to the End of the World.

It's not necessary to go to the polar regions to find places called the End of the World. Apart from Land's End in Cornwall there's a World's End in West London, another in North Wales, and probably many more in remote country areas. Ours is in Europe, though only just, but it has a much greater claim than most to the title The End of the World .

LIST OF RECIPES

Part one

FROM WALES TO THE END OF THE WORLD

\ CHAPTER 1

"Grub first, then ethics"

Berthold Brecht

West Wales: immigrants and organic growers

THIS IS an ancient and settled land. Across the valley, on the south facing slopes of Cwm Mabws there's a flat-topped tumulus covered in gorse where I suspect people of the Bronze Age buried their dead. Down the valley a little further the Celts left a conspicuous sign of their settlement, and despite centuries of agriculture and a recently constructed golf course the concentric earthworks of their defende settlement still dominate the hilltop of Pen-rhos. So when Rhys ap Gruffydd granted Cwm Mabws and the lands of Llanrhystud to the Knights Hospitallers of St John in the twelfth century the valley had already been settled and farmed for centuries.

On clear days right down the valley there is a triangular glimpse of the sea, and when it is really fine you can see Ynys Enlli, Bardsey Island, on the horizon. These sightings of Bardsey and Llŷn, the Lleyn peninsula, help us to read the weather but the island represents something else for me and whenever I catch sight of it I remember a naturalist from North Wales and a trip to a more distant sunny island in 1975.

It was at this time that I really started to consider leaving metropolitan life and wondered if it would be possible to make a living from the land somewhere in the countryside. After many false starts this train of thought became a chain of events that led eventually in late 1976 to Ty'n yr Helyg, a small farm near Llanrhystud overlooking Cwm Mabws.

Perhaps the greatest impetus to move from London came from the series of warm dry summers that culminated that year in the long drought. Although the rivers ran dry and the hillsides were brown through lack of rain, the stone built farmhouse seemed deliciously cool and refreshing after the murderous heat of my attic flat in London. We finally made the move in October, and even the autumn deluge that followed didn't douse our enthusiasm since it brought its own magic. As the heavy rains soaked into the sun-warmed soil the surrounding fields erupted with field mushrooms, giant puff-balls, parasols and horse mushrooms; an endless feast of edible fungi that has yet to be repeated.

In the first months there were many visits from erstwhile colleagues and acquaintances from London who tended to stick their feet under our dining table and whilst tucking into the fruits of the first meagre harvest from our kitchen garden would ask with exaggerated scepticism, *"Do you really think you can be self-sufficient?"* The way to deal with this was to serve up bowls of nettle soup, fried puff-balls and steamed chickweed and to offer dandelion coffee with goat's milk. After such a menu few sceptics wanted to return for another visit.

One of the frequent surprises that came in that first year was the discovery that many other people of my generation were making a career break and moving to the country, often with the intention of growing fruit and vegetables organically. Unknown to me, Barbara and her elder brother Hubert were in this self-same year moving away from their home town of Nuremberg and buying a house deep in the south German countryside where, with a small community of people, they would grow vegetables, learn carpentry and pottery, and hold regular summer music festivals. It was something of an international phenomenon. In Germany they coined the word *aussteiger* to describe people who deserted their professional lives, whereas in Britain we were all lumped together as 'drop-outs' and 'hippies'. Across the Atlantic there was a parallel movement underway and in the cult sixties film *Easy Rider* the two bikers come across a community of new farmers in the desert. "I wonder if they'll make it" mutters Dennis Hopper. "They'll make it" says Peter Fonda grittily, putting on his shades and kicking the bike into life. By the 1970s these early initiatives had become an organic farming movement, as the Californian writer and farmer Michael Ableman says:

"I began farming because I wanted to eat well and to tend the earth. I didn't know that I was part of a movement. It was years before I found others who were working the same way, calling their practices 'organic', 'sustainable', 'natural', and even 'sensible' agriculture."

In Wales, my own feelings about this were less positive than Michael Ableman's. I didn't want to be part of a movement, and I wrote rather testily at the time,

"You know, I can't figure it out. There we were in London looking for a place to live in the country and after all sorts of attempts and odd coincidences we find this place in Wales. Just four people finding a place on their own in the empty countryside. But what happens? We end up part of a bloody social movement, a geographical movement, an exodus! The hills are teeming with Londoners, drop out sociology teachers, ex-social-workers, and all sorts of no-hopers left over from the sixties peace and love brigade. Presumably they all made individual decisions. They didn't all get together one day in Portobello Road and choose to come down in a bloody charabanc. How does it happen?"

Before the move I remember visualizing the countryside and the house, the rows of crops I would grow, the gardens I would create, and the evening tables full of food and drink we would sit around. But, strangely, I never thought of the community of people I might be joining. Socially Wales was *tabula rasa* and it wasn't until a year later when I started learning Welsh in Llangwyryfon School, at evening classes taught by Mari Llwyd, Sue Rhys and Peter Lord, that the issues started to emerge. Without realising it, we had moved from England to a country with a distinct language and culture where many things rankled, – not only from ancient, but also from recent history. As Professor Gwyn Williams put it at the time:

"There is Tryweryn and the drowning of Welsh valleys to provide water for England; the refusal of the Post Office to issue stamps to commemorate the Welsh Bible in 1970 and

the fiftieth anniversary of Urdd Gobaith Cymru...the tearing apart of Welsh skies by low-flying jets and by Concorde...the continued upkeep of a war machine which costs Wales about £200 million a year...the pros and cons of the relationship between conservation and industry...unease over the buying up of cottages and small-holdings by well-to-do outsiders..."

During our evening discussions Peter Lord put the question most aggressively, *"What right do you have to come and live here?"* Now, as then, I find this a hard question to answer, mostly because I don't think in these terms; I mean, from what authority can you derive a right to live anywhere? As a car sticker we picked up in Germany says, *'Wir alle sind auslander – denk nach'* (We're all foreigners – think about it).

My primary concern has been to try to understand why and how events occur rather than to make a moral assessment. Yet with nationalism and ethnicity such increasingly potent forces, the question has refused to go away. In fact, although there are farms in Wales which have been in the same family for generations, and although there are individuals with light hair and eye colouring that suggests a genetic link right back to the earliest Celtic settlers, history shows that there have been continual movements of peoples and ethnic groups throughout the country. For example, although Barbara is from distant Franconia in southern Germany there were Ffrancs (or Franks) in Wales centuries ago who came as mercenaries and are mentioned in ninth century Welsh poetry and who left their mark in place names like Nant Ffrancon. As David Jenkins has shown in his study of the agricultural community of South-west Wales the concept of the 'family farm' can be rather misleading if it is taken to mean a farm handed down regularly from one generation to another. Certainly in the nineteenth and early twentieth century people moved regularly from one tenancy to another as circumstances required and as landlords permitted, so only the term 'family farm' remains, a useful term to describe a farm worked by a family rather than by outside labour.

The small wave of immigrants of which I was a part in the mid 1970s came to settle, to farm, to garden and to produce crops just as many previous groups have done over the millennia. What we found was a countryside that had changed little in recent centuries, where the agricultural potential is severely limited by thin, silty and acidic soils, high rainfall, poor drainage, and salt-laden winds driving in from Cardigan Bay. Few of those of us who planned to grow vegetables were aware of these limitations, and we were ignorant of the fact that they had largely confined local agriculture to arable and self-sufficient pastoral farming for at least the last five hundred years. As recently as the 1950s farms like Ty'n yr Helyg were still worked by horse power. They kept cows, sheep and pigs and where conditions allowed they grew cabbages, potatoes, carrots and swedes. D Parry Jones describes how his father in South Wales was amazed during the early years of the Second World War when a field that took him a good three weeks to plough with horses was finished in one day with a tractor, a field he had worked for fifty years; and David Jenkins reports that, *"In 1953 I counted thirty five people engaged in the hay harvest of an 8 acre holding. They worked from midday till seven o'clock in the evening with none of the equipment that has long been common on larger holdings…During the summer of 1959 I watched men cutting corn with a scythe and binding it by hand in a north Cardiganshire valley within twelve miles of Aberystwyth. As late as 1951 the reaping hook was used in mid Cardiganshire to save the crop during a difficult harvest."*

By the 1970s mechanisation of farm work had reached just about all of the farms in Cardiganshire, although my neighbour Richard Moore Colyer saw the reaping hook used at Ystumtuen in 1973. Further changes were beginning to occur also as the carrots and sticks of, first national, and then European Community economic and agricultural policy pushed farming in the direction of larger, more specialised and thus, supposedly, more cost effective and efficient units. One consequence was fewer people employed on the land: there was a 'Payment to Outgoers Scheme' and some farmhouses became redundant as the lands of neighbouring farms were amalgamated with grant aid. Many of these properties were sold off with just the minimum of land to make them attractive to buyers. It was these, and the smaller, less favoured and therefore cheaper farms, that were bought by the new organic farmers and gardeners arriving in Wales with that mood of enthusiasm for the rural, self-sufficient good life that pervaded the time. As the new immigrants moved into 'unmodernised' and often derelict farmhouses and cottages, many locals must have felt the nostalgia of Glyn Jones who remembered with love and sadness the place in north Wales where he was born; *"the memories flooding back as I look at the places where the house, smithy and outhouses used to stand. All that is left of the old stone buildings is a small piece of the 'ty bach' ..., which served the family as the outside lavatory, and the crumbling walls of the building where the cattle and other animals were housed during the winter."*

During the first few years we were at Ty'n yr Helyg there was an annual visit from two elderly ladies who made the pilgrimage to see their childhood home at nearby Ysgubor Fach, a cottage uninhabited for over fifty years, by now derelict and serving merely as a winter shelter for horses and cattle. After a while I noticed that these pilgrimages had ceased, and the two women probably never saw the rehabilitation of the old cottage they had loved as it was rebuilt by an Englishman from Yorkshire in the late 1970s.

Organic farming and gardening

DESPITE ITS limited agricultural potential the West Wales area has nonetheless achieved a considerable reputation for organic food production since the 1970s. In some cases, most notably Brynllys in Borth, it has been based on a traditional Welsh family farm, while other enterprises have been the work of newcomers. In many ways the area has been a hotbed of organic initiatives, from the demonstration gardens at the Centre for Alternative Technology at Corris, near

Machynlleth, to Organic Farm Foods' vegetable packhouse in Lampeter. To call it a hotbed is to use an old cliché, but it is an apt one because generations of gardeners used the hotbed as a means of raising delicate crops under difficult conditions. Organic farmers and vegetable growers in West Wales were the first to form British Organic Farmers and the Organic Growers' Association, and there have been scores of other initiatives involving cheese and yogurt makers, organic free range egg producers, smallholders, garlic growers, beekeepers and honey producers, compost manufacturers, plant raisers, nurseries, and organic livestock farmers. Like crops transplanted from a hotbed some have survived and flourished, but many too have wilted and died in the recent harsh economic climate.

Certainly the recession years of 1991 to 1993 took their toll of organic growers' businesses, just as they hit all sectors of the economy. Many small-scale growers made heavy personal and financial investments in their holdings during the 1980s, spurred on by the enthusiastic demand for their produce. In truth the real costs of production were seldom passed on to the consumer, and when the recession came and demand faltered, many growers found themselves over-borrowed at the bank and facing high mortgage interest rates and finance costs. Moreover they were faced with a reduction in their capital base as the real value of their land and property fell, together with lower prices for their produce. It is a situation I've seen repeated throughout Wales and the border counties, and the reaction amongst those growers who have stayed in business has been either to specialise and to grow fewer crops on a larger scale for wholesaling, or to move into direct market schemes, delivering boxes of their organically grown vegetables directly to consumers.

As Nic Lampkin of the University of Wales, Aberystwyth, has pointed out in his book on organic farming, many of the people who started farming organically in the 1960s and 70s were newcomers to farming and faced many of the problems which any newcomer would face. He continues, *"But those early pioneers now have a wealth of experience and many are as hardheaded as any commercial farmer trying to make a go of things. More importantly, they have been supplemented in the 1980s by an increasing number of conventional farmers with existing practical experience who are better placed, both financially and practically, to make the changeover.*"

The basic aim of organic growing is to produce food by methods that improve and maintain the fertility of the soil without the use of artificial fertilisers, and without recourse to synthetic chemical sprays in the control of weeds, pests and diseases. The goal is a self-sustaining system which produces food rich in nutrients and without toxic chemical residues. The methods employed by farmers and growers to achieve these aims and goals include building soil fertility with composts and animal manures; crop rotations; cultivations that maintain good soil structure; and mechanical or biological methods of weed, pest and disease control. The organic ideal is a mixed farm with livestock incorporated into the growing system and with fields rested from intensive cropping by periods of fertility-building where the land is grazed and manured by animals. In some ways this is very similar to the farming methods that were traditional to the mixed family farms of West Wales, but the difference in the approach of many of the new arrivals in the 1970s and thereafter lies in the range of crops that have been grown. Not content with potatoes, carrots and swedes, the organic growers have attempted all manner of crops: lettuces and salads; calabrese; spinach; oriental crops like chinese leaves; mediterranean crops such as courgettes; and in greenhouses and polythene growing houses beside tomatoes and cucumbers, I've seen crops of capsicum and aubergines. Despite the fact that the area is at the very northern limit of their range, french beans, fennel, and celeriac have all been produced, whilst here and there I've also come across the occasional crop of asparagus, sweetcorn and chilli peppers. At Ty'n yr Helyg we were not alone in planting gooseberry and currant bushes, apple, pear and plum trees and in growing strawberries and raspberries. And although it is not perhaps too surprising that grapes and figs are grown on the coast at

Aberaeron, I've also eaten figs grown near Nebo at the foot of Mynydd Bach in the Cambrian Mountains and seen peaches growing, admittedly in a greenhouse, at over a thousand feet in nearby Trefenter.

In our own gardens we grew crops primarily to sell locally at the Market Hall in Aberystwyth, in our Salad Shop, and to many local hotels and restaurants. But we also sent produce out of the area: lettuces, cabbages, tomatoes, cucumbers, courgettes and swedes have gone via Organic Farm Foods in Lampeter to the major supermarket chains in England, and for several years we sent herbs and unusual salad and vegetable crops to the wholesale market in Birmingham. So for fifteen years we grew a very wide range of fruit and vegetables, some years as many as forty different lines. Even when growing such a large range, however, local growers are at a disadvantage because there is a paradox that has arisen from the abundance of choice that consumers have grown to expect: when crops are in season, and in plentiful supply from local growers, demand falls and prices are at their very lowest.

What has happened is that as the large multiple chains have come to dominate the retailing of fresh produce so they have become very skilled at sourcing supplies of fruit and vegetables from all over the globe to provide a year round continuity of supply. It is an area where competition between stores has been very keen and some larger scale British vegetable growers have sought to stay in the game by extending their growing season by using carefully controlled greenhouse conditions with artificial growing media like rockwool, atmospheres enriched with CO_2, computerised heating systems, and supplementary ultra violet lighting. The most enterprising have also invested in the fastest growing vegetable areas of Spain and Portugal to provide their customers with out of season produce. In fact by the 1980s the Almeria region of Spain was the fastest growing horticultural region in Europe, with water pumped up from artesian wells to irrigate the arid land, vast areas of which are now covered by polythene growing tunnels and shade houses. Much of the investment for this development came from highly successful horticultural companies in the Netherlands, and elsewhere EC grants have encouraged local growers to specialize. Specialization is inevitable given the pressures to supply the large marketing companies. The problem is that it results in monoculture and can leave the growers much more vulnerable to crop failure, or to the fickleness of the market, than when they grew a range of crops. During a visit to the tiny Canary Island of La Palma, for example, I learned that growers receive grants to grow bananas for export to Spain and elsewhere in the EC. So, increasingly, they are giving up the mixed cropping of potatoes, avocados, papayas, and pineapples to concentrate on bananas. Just as agricultural policy in Wales has led to the decline of the mixed family farm and the dominance of monocultures like sheep farming, so the process of specialization continues even in (what seems to us) remote areas like La Palma.

The downside of this specialized growing to produce abundance for consumers throughout the year is the loss of excitement that comes with the arrival of new season crops after a period when they've not been available. Once, for example, the arrival of the first new potatoes from Pembrokeshire in late May and early June was associated with real excitement and they commanded high prices. Now new potatoes are available most of the year, and Pembrokes follow a long list of imports starting around Christmas from Italy, then, Cyprus, Spain, the Canaries, Jersey and Brittany.

Fruit and vegetables lose vitamins quickly after harvest, and quality deteriorates during long periods of transport. For this reason post harvest fungicides, waxes and irradiation are used to protect produce, and to promote its apparent freshness. This is particularly true of produce imported from overseas, especially from tropical countries; so the issue of food quality is not just about the methods of production, but includes post harvest treatments. Proponents of in-season organically grown vegetables point to the poor flavour of many crops grown under intensive conditions, and to the lack of vitamins and mineral trace elements which seem to be associated with crops grown with chemical fertilisers, pesticides and fungicides. Researchers in Germany found, for example, that vegetables grown organically have, on the one hand, higher amounts of desirable proteins, ascorbic acid (vitamin C), carbohydrates and minerals, while, on the other hand they have lower levels of undesirable nitrates and sodium chloride.

In Britain the Ministry of Agriculture's Working Party on Pesticide Residues issues an annual report on tests carried out on home grown and imported fruit and vegetables. Carrots have been a great cause for concern especially over the levels of organo-phosphorous insecticides where residues of carrot fly control products have been found in significant levels. A Ministry survey in 1991 found that the residue levels of triazophos, a contact and stomach acting organophosphorous insecticide, exceeded the Maximum Residue Level in nearly half the samples. These findings confirmed those from studies in 1989 and 1990, but as there was no evidence to suggest excessive pesticide misuse, the Maximum Residue Level for the product Hostathion, which is based on triazophos, was increased tenfold in the 1994 Pesticides (maximum levels in crops and feeding stuffs) Regulation. Even if the original level was set particularly low, in the present climate of pesticide use it is very unusual for the ministry to raise Maximum Residue Levels. In view of widespread concern about health risks posed by organo-phosphorous compounds, and pesticide residues in general, raising of permitted levels tenfold reflected the effect of the campaign mounted by scientists and growers, and the interests of the chemical companies, rather than those of the consumers.

By 1995, however, the Government was forced to accept that a limit to the use of organophosphorous sprays had to be introduced since, "unexpectedly high residues of acutely toxic pesticides in some individual carrots had been found". In fact surveys in 1994 showed that within some fields, although some carrots were within 'safe' limits, others were not. Between one and two per cent of individual carrot roots contained residues as many as 25 times greater than expected, with

50 per cent of individual carrots from some locations exceeding Acceptable Daily Intake (ADI) residues by up to three times.

In consequence, the Food Minister, Angela Browning, announced control measures which included a limit of three organo-phosphorous treatments per crop per year. It also became government advice to prepare carrots by cutting off the top 2.3 millimetres and peeling them.

As the problem surfaced in the national press, commentators like Joanna Blythman, writing in the *Guardian Weekend* magazine, concluded that, *"a very serious problem has been identified in British carrots – with possible implications for all other crops which have not yet been tested on an individual basis"* and she proposed that, *"a wholesale change to organic methods is, of course, the only total answer to the current problem."*

The danger is that root crops, like carrots, may absorb residues from the regular applications of pesticide that they receive during their long growing season, and become a chemical 'sink'. In the case of salad crops and fruit, however, it is the interval between spraying with pesticides and harvest that represents most cause for concern. As a general precaution all fruit and salads that are to be eaten raw should be well washed to remove as much pesticide residue as possible.

Ministry tests on winter grown greenhouse lettuces revealed a worrying spate of pesticide misuse in 1992, with residues of two pesticides, chlorothalin and vinclozolin, neither of which are officially approved for use in the UK; and in blackcurrant samples as many as four different pesticide residues were found in some home grown fruit. In view of the large quantities of blackcurrant juice that children drink, the Working Party decided to continue to monitor residues in the fruit.

In December 1994 a fruit grower in Penrith, Cumbria was fined almost a thousand pounds after a test for pesticide residues found DDT levels in a sample of blackcurrants that could only have resulted from a recent application, even though DDT had, in fact, been banned in Britain a decade earlier in 1984. DDT and other organo-chlorides like lindane, dieldrin, and aldrin were amongst the first mass produced pesticides and are particularly harmful because they tend to collect in fatty tissue and do not readily break down. They accumulate in food chains, passing from insects to birds, to fish and finally to larger mammals, including humans. After a voluntary ban between 1974 and 1978 organo-chlorides were finally banned by law because of their toxicity, environmental persistence and effects on wildlife.

Agriculture and the countryside

APART FROM the issue of food quality another central argument in favour of organic growing concerns the effect of agriculture on the environment. Increasingly in recent years organic farmers and growers have been finding common cause with other groups concerned with ecology and conservation. Since we don't use biocides there is less of a direct threat to wildlife on organic farms, and the regulations in organic agriculture that require the conservation of herb rich meadows, hedgerows, wetlands and woodlands result in a diversity of wildlife habitats that reward the farmer with shelter belts and a 'beetle bank' of beneficial insects to pollinate crops and to control pests like aphids. The penalty is the loss of acreage that we could otherwise plough and intensively crop. The more evidence becomes available of the destructive effect of intensive agriculture on the environment and wildlife, the more public opinion and ultimately government policy comes to recognize the need for a change in approach.

Recent evidence of the degradation of the environment comes from the 1990 countryside survey which covers a twelve year period and graphically illustrates the loss of plant species, hedgerows, dry stone walls, ponds, and woods throughout Britain. Although the survey did not set out to discover why these changes were occurring, most commentators agree that the intensification of farming throughout the 1980s with the associated heavy use of machinery, fertiliser and pesticides is the prime suspect, along with air pollution due to the burning of coal, petrol and gas.

The worst losses of plant species and wildlife habitats were in the arable areas of eastern Britain. In 1990 some arable fields had 25 per cent fewer 'weed' species than in 1978 which, of course, meant a reduced level of food and shelter for birds and insects.

Not that in west Wales there is any room for complacency. In the quite recent past agricultural policy favoured draining wetlands, 'improving' grassland by ploughing out herb-rich pasture and replacing it with uniform ryegrasses, grubbing out hedges to create larger enclosures; and of course large tracts of Wales have been planted with sitka spruce in place of indigenous broad-leaved woodlands. Ecologists stress the importance of bio-diversity and west Wales is rich in quite distinct habitats and environments including wooded valleys like Cwm Mabws, the cliffs, beaches and estuaries of the coastline, the lowland agricultural 'barley belt', temperate rainforests, wetlands, moorlands, coniferous forests and the Cambrian mountains: a diversity the importance of which is hard to overemphasize. In Cardigan Bay there are seals and bottle nosed dolphins, though their numbers are greatly reduced compared to the great fishing days of the eighteenth and nineteenth centuries when contemporary reports speak of shoals of bottlenoses and porpoises being run on shore and used to make oil. Now pollution is added to the threat of over fishing in Cardigan Bay.

North of Aberystwyth, Cors Fochno (or Borth Bog) is the largest remaining coastal raised bog in Europe and one of the largest inland raised bogs lies only a few miles away to the east, near Tregaron. The area has the highest density of ravens in Europe and the red kite has staged a comeback from near extinction in the late 1970s so that there are now about 500, more than that most Welsh of hawks, the merlin. The debate about farming, food and the environment has become increasingly serious and it is particularly significant that this area is the only one in the country to have an MP who stood as a joint candidate for both the Welsh Nationalist Party, Plaid Cymru, and the Green Party. For organic farmers and growers, however, the level of support in the Government's Organic Aid Scheme announced in 1993 was pitifully inadequate and much lower than comparable subsidies in other European countries introduced under the EC's Agri-environment Programme.

The taste of Wales

FOOD QUALITY and concern for the environment are the two issues that underpinned our commitment to organic growing, but there is another benefit – that of flavour. There is widespread agreement that although a huge range of fruit and vegetables is now abundantly available throughout the year, somehow taste and flavour have been lost. There are quite clear reasons for this. Lack of freshness is one; the use of varieties grown only for yield is another. Then there's the heavy use of fertilisers that increase yield by the uptake of water, again at the expense of flavour. Our own approach was to concentrate on growing vegetables where freshness is at a premium, since we live in an area which is quite remote from the major areas of horticultural production. This meant leafy crops like spinach and broccoli and, above all, salads.

Curiously our Salad Shop had its origins in a series of crop failures in 1985. That summer we had planted out a number of late salad crops that failed fully to mature, and we couldn't really sell them. Joy Larkcom's book, *The Salad Garden,* provided an answer: to use these salads in a mixed pack marketed as saladini. These mixed packs proved a great success, one that was repeated in 1986, and so when shop premises became available near our stall in Aberystwyth's Market Hall we decided to go for a shop that concentrated upon salads, and to make take-away prepared salads a key feature. We drew upon our influences and experiences in choosing which crops to grow and sell, which herbs and dressings to use, and how best to combine textures and colours in making salads. The shop was also stocked with the produce of local dairy farms: butter, cream, yogurt, and a variety of Welsh cheeses, plus local honey, Welsh made mustard and local free range eggs when available. Eventually we also stocked organic meat: lamb from our own flock of Llanwenog sheep, beef and locally made burgers, free range chickens from Craig Farm in Powys, and bacon and sausages from Welsh pigs. Some of the most popular of these were the bratwurst wholemeat sausages made for us locally to a south German recipe supplied by Barbara's father.

Perhaps one of the most rewarding responses to the enterprise was the frequently repeated remark that the shop looked, smelt and felt like a continental food shop. This was especially gratifying since, by harvesting herbs, salads and flowers daily for our shop, and by arranging supplies from other local farmers and growers, we tried to continue locally the rich tradition of European food and farming we have experienced beyond west Wales.

CHAPTER 2

The German influence: Franconia and South Tyrol

ALTHOUGH GROWING vegetables in west Wales has been the predominant influence on our attitude to food and diet, there have been many others, and Franconia is one of the strongest. Barbara grew up in this Celtic enclave in northern Bavaria where, near the town of Nuremberg, her family run a restaurant which specialises in seasonal menus with fresh fish and game, local vegetables, herbs, fruit and wine. Before I met Barbara and visited the *Gasthaus* I had little idea of German food, apart from sausage and sauerkraut. Like many of my generation I'd taken every travel opportunity to go south to the Mediterranean, and I'd looked primarily to France for cultural and culinary inspiration, so the *Gasthaus* experience became something of a challenge to the hegemony of French cuisine.

Nuremberg and Franconia
Although once a Celtic region, Franconia derives its name from the Franks, and at the time of the Second Reich the first Diet of the Holy Roman Empire was held in the ancient town of Nuremberg. The walled town, with its imposing central castle, dominates the single sandstone hill in a large plain, and hence its name: *"Nur Ein Berg"*, "only one hill". The Holy Roman Emperor Charlemagne made the first divisions of the town into parishes and lodged them with the Pope who was then in Avignon. Copies of these remain in the French city, and they still correspond quite closely to today's civil divisions.

In the 13th century Nuremberg became a *Freie Riechstadte,* or free imperial city, independent both of Northern Prussia and the Southern Austro-Hungarian Empire. The town grew rich in the middle ages from its strategic geographical position commanding the north-south trade routes, and tolls were exacted from spice merchants and other travelling traders. As the town prospered great families like the Patricias became patrons of the arts. The painter Albrecht Dürer lived and worked here as a goldsmith and etcher and so did the stonemason Veit Stoss, the woodcutter Michael Volgemutt and the sculptors Adam Kraft and Peter Fisher. It was in Nuremberg that Peter Henlein invented the first portable clock, a pocket watch the size and shape of an egg; and it was here also that Martin Behaim, after the voyages of Columbus and Magellan, made the first globe. Music also flourished, especially in the fifteenth and sixteenth centuries, and this, of course, was the home of the shoemaker and poet, Hans Sachs, the central figure of Wagner's *Die Meistersinger von Nürnberg*.

The Third Reich left marks on Nuremberg as indelible as those of the Second Reich. The Nazi party held rallies here in 1926 and Hitler's 1934 rally was recorded in Leni Reifenstahl's remarkable film *The Triumph of the Will*. The scene of the rallies at the Zeppelin fields remains; Albert Speer's monoliths posed too great a problem to demolish and for decades this was a taboo area visited only by GIs to play squash. In the 1970s the Zeppelin fields were used for rock concerts, first by Santana and then in 1978 (although he had vowed never to play in Germany) by Bob Dylan. Now circuses come here and in the summer there are fairs.

During the Second World War Nuremberg was devastated by allied bombing, but the medieval and Renaissance buildings have been skillfully reconstructed and only the photographs inside the churches and at the Germanishes Museum attest to the extent of the destruction. All of the old town is now pedestrianised and the main places of interest can be reached on foot. It is also a shoppers' paradise. At Frauenkirche there's a huge open air market place with stalls loaded with fruit and vegetables. At twelve noon the church bells of Frauenkirche chime and the *glockenspiele* revolves to reveal the figures of the Emperor Charles IV and seven electors of the Holy Roman Empire. It is here in

December that the famous *Christkindl Markt* is held. The fresh produce stalls selling geese and ducks, fruit, vegetables, herbs, flowers and plants are pushed to the outskirts of the market square and the *Christkindl Markt* itself is devoted to all the distinctive items of a South German Christmas: the traditional cakes *Lebkuchen* and *Stöllen*; *Zwetschgenmannle* the little figures made from dried prunes; straw stars; pottery and jewellery, sugared almonds and marzipan figures and everywhere the air full of the aroma of barbecued *bratwurst*. You buy them in a bread roll or brotchen from one of the countless stalls to eat wandering the Mart, to be followed by a mug of *gluhwein* and some sugared almonds from a paper cone.

Food and drink in Franconia

The area surrounding Nuremberg is favoured with light sandy soils that grow excellent crops, especially in the intensively cultivated region near the airport known as *Knoblauchsland* (garlic land). Vineyards lie to the south and the nearby forests are rich in game.

The wines are scarcely known outside Germany, since, like many other countries, the best wines are kept for home consumption and large quantities of sweet, poor quality Liebfraumilch and Rheinhessen are exported to Britain. The reds in particular are hardly ever seen in the UK yet some of the Barrique red wines, matured in oak casks, rival the best that Bordeaux can offer; but it's the Franconian white wines that represent the widest range of vintages. For these the most widely grown grapes are, in order of harvest, Riesling, Silvaner and Muller Thurgau. Riesling has the reputation as the finest grape but the slightly less flowery Silvaner produces some excellent dry wines. Muller Thurgau is a hybrid grape bred around 1920 by Herr Muller of Thurgau in Switzerland by crossing Riesling (M) with Silvaner (F). The *Qualitats* wines are bottled at the vineyards and classified according to the level of natural fruit sugar in the grape. A normal quality QBA table wine has 70% fruit sugar, the minimum permitted level. Next comes *Kabinette* with 75%, then *Spatlese* 80%, *Auslese* 90%, *Beerenauslese* 100%. *Trockenbeerauslese* has 120%. This last wine is made at the end of the grape harvest when the fruit fly has virtually dried the grapes of any water content and they've been withered by autumn frosts. The white wines are bottled in the distinctive semi-circular *bocksbeutel*, and the best are matured in 750 or 700 ml bottles. When the first grapes are harvested much earlier in the year the vineyards sell *federweisser* which is made from the very first pressings of the grapes and is drunk straight away. It's rich in natural yeasts and fruit sugars but low in alcohol, very cloudy and musty and prized as a health drink, very good for the stomach, for digestion and as a diuretic.

The beer of the area is much better known outside the region than the wine, and it is the essential drink to wash down *bratwurst*, the spicy, wholemeat pork sausages that, in Nuremberg, are best eaten at the *Bratwursthausle* in the town centre near the castle, where they're barbecued and served with *sauerkraut* and potato salad.

Game and hunting

Mention game and hunting in Britain and hackles soon rise because hunting is synonymous with fox hunting, the 'sport' that Oscar Wilde described as the unspeakable in full pursuit of the uneatable. In Franconia hunting or *Jagen* is more akin to gamekeeping, and the hunter or *Jäger* makes an arrangement with farmers to control those animals that are liable to damage crops: deer, pigeon, hares, rabbits, wild boar, pheasants and partridges. At most restaurants in Britain and the rest of Europe, and certainly those we have supplied with vegetables in West Wales, when there's game on the menu its usually the farmed variety supplied in exact cuts and joints and vacuum packed. After a hunt in Franconia the scene in the Gasthaus kitchen could not provide a greater contrast. Villagers pluck partridge and pheasant whilst sides of venison hang in the cool room, and all of the game is used, not just the choicest cuts. Pâtés are made from the livers, brawn from other offal and the bones are rendered down for gravies and sauces. For many people however, this sort of tradition is no longer politically correct or morally acceptable. The killing of wildlife for food is seen as unnecessary and barbaric. The use of locally killed game is confined to fewer and fewer kitchens and is replaced by the products of intensive agriculture.

There's a corruption of values in the way we've rejected the use of wild animals for food yet replaced it with an often repulsive system of factory farming which too often involves cruelty to animals and pollution of the environment. What has changed, and what has been lost, is the traditional relationship between the control of game that threatens crops and a source of local food. The situation with freshwater fish is rather similar. Whereas tickled trout were once a common country treat, and the stewpond in the country estate or monastery supplied the great kitchens with carp, now the lakes and rivers are fished for sport and fish farms supply most of the trout, carp and salmon that finds its way to the table. In Franconia one of the great delicacies in the restaurant are *krebs* (crayfish) which cost about ten pounds a kilo collected from a fish farm. In former times the *krebs* were cheap protein especially for those country people without their own animals; once they were caught for free in the streams and brooks, now they're a treat for the very rich.

Gasthaus Rottner

The restaurant was originally a farmhouse that became a country inn. When the family went to work in the fields they left food for guests, and as the town of Nuremberg grew their country inn, called Gasthaus Zur Grünnen Weintraube (The Green Grape), in the village of Grossreuth became a popular place for families to visit on Sunday trips to the countryside. In the post war period the town continued to grow, surrounding the village and commandeering farm land for new housing. As urban growth gobbled up their fields the restaurant grew at the expense of the farm, but the family retained as much of the land as they could and continued to grow a field of asparagus, and, next to the kitchen, they cultivated a large garden where herbs, salads, vegetables and flowers continue to be grown for the restaurant. All the apprentice cooks learn from their first day how to identify the fresh herbs growing in the garden and to know what crops are in season. Each morning one of them has the job of going to the garden to cut fresh herbs for the day's menu, and flowers are picked to decorate the dining rooms. During our frequent visits we join trips to collect rosehips, sloes and elderberries for making sauces and syrups, and make the rounds of vineyards, farms and fishponds to collect supplies.

The style and cuisine of the restaurant is based on the use of produce from local fields, woods and streams to provide seasonal delicacies. Traditionally the spring menu started with hop-shoots and 'well cress' (similar to water cress), and a sorrel or asparagus soup. The main dishes were asparagus (served either as a salad or hot with butter), sausage, ham, pigeon, or the seasonal speciality of roast kid. Between courses there was rhubarb sorbet and then a dessert of elderflower fritters or fresh strawberries. In summer the first mushrooms, ceps and redcaps appeared on the menu, with chervil soup or dumplings with fresh parsley, to be followed by fresh water crayfish, trout in Franconian wine bouillon, or fried pike. Summer saw the first venison and duck and, for dessert, cherry fritters with sage leaves or *fraises de bois* (wild strawberries). In the autumn the kitchen offered snails in sourdough rolls, smoked frog legs, and vegetable soup; there were freshwater eels, young wild duck, partridge, pheasant and hare, with desserts of fresh blackberries and raspberries, plums in red wine, apple fritters and apple ice cream. In the winter the specialities were gooseliver sausage, spiced game soup, carp baked in lard, wild boar, and sucking pig, with goose at Christmas time. The special winter desserts were rum compote and *Kartauser,* which are sweet dumplings made from white bread soaked in milk then deep fried in breadcrumbs with sugar and cinnamon.

In recent years, with Barbara's younger brother Stefan taking over as head chef, there have been some changes to this traditional menu, but the basic philosophy remains unchanged. Snails, frog legs and sucking pig may have gone and the influence of modern culinary ideas has made an impact, but the commitment to local seasonal produce is still fundamental. The meal we had following the christening of Stefan's son, Valentin, gives a flavour of how the traditions are blended with modern cooking. After cocktails of *Sekt* (German champagne) with orange juice and campari, we started the lunch with a first course of soup, a clear consommé with dumplings of liver pâté and bread and strips of pancake. This was followed by deep fried carp with potato salad, lambs' lettuce, and celeriac salad. Whereas these two courses had been versions of Franconian classics, the dessert showed the full influence of nouvelle cuisine. It was a beautifully arranged plate of fruits, plum terrine, pear with almond and elderberry sauce with an almond ice stuffing, a sauce of mangoes and whinberries, plum and almond parfait, plum fritter (with the plum stone replaced by an almond), almond ice cream and the whole plate garnished with slices of fresh plum and lemon balm leaves.

Nouvelle cuisine

In the 1970s and 1980s the growing concern with healthy eating had an impact on the dominant tradition of French Grande Cuisine. In France chefs like Michel Guérard refined traditional recipes to produce lighter meals with a greater emphasis on natural flavours than on heavy sauces made by hours of simmering, the legacy of Escoffier. The ideas of cuisine *minceur* and *nouvelle* cuisine spread throughout Europe, emphasising the importance of fresh ingredients and the minimal use of fats, starches and sugars. Fresh fruits were now used for sweetening and puréed vegetables replaced flour to thicken sauces. Also, young baby vegetables were served whole after the minimum of cooking and presentation became very important, well balanced meals being obliged to have a blend of attractive colours and flavours. In the late 1980s top chefs like Ian

McAndrew were complaining that in Britain it was difficult to buy small, young, fresh vegetables in the *nouvelle* cuisine style. McAndrew was even thrown off a pick-your-own farm in England for picking undersized courgettes.

One autumn, around this time, we were asked by a local restaurant near Aberystwyth to supply fruit and vegetables for the meals to be provided at a seminar run by Food from Britain. The restaurant wanted to use exclusively local Welsh produce. Enthusiastically we suggested leeks, spinach, and turnips, which were all in season in our fields, and Bramley cooking apples and elderberries from the orchard and hedgerows. Unfortunately these seasonal vegetables didn't seem to have the kudos that was required and we eventually spent a nerve racking late October afternoon going through the polytunnels looking for baby courgettes en fleur, and late fruiting strawberries that hadn't succumbed to botrytis. We also had to sort through carrots to find small roots that could pass as 'baby' carrots. 'Baby' vegetables is another corrupted idea. Originally in *nouvelle* cuisine the idea was to use young vegetables at the peak of their flavour, rather than to leave them to mature as the commercial grower usually does to achieve maximum weight and yield. Sadly 'baby' became synonymous with 'small' rather than 'young', and so our local chef overlooked the young, seasonal leeks and turnips in favour of the simply small but older carrots. (It should in fairness be added that this particular restaurant subsequently became a regular user of baby leeks and was the most enthusiastic local buyer of our salad crops and fresh fruit).

For me the Franconian influence has been to emphasise the rich tradition of European cooking at a time when there is a general enthusiasm for exotic cooking and imported produce from all quarters of the globe. One of the disadvantages of this trend is the neglect of the marvellous food possibilities that lie at our doorstep: in our gardens and in the meadows and hedgerows. Another serious disadvantage lies in the fact that third world farmers are being pressurised to grow cash crops for export to Western markets rather than the staple foodstuffs necessary to feed the undernourished multitudes in their own countries.

In our shop we tried to continue the tradition by harvesting herbs, salads and flowers daily and by arranging supplies from other local farmers and growers, in just the same way that the restaurant is run by the Rottner family in Franconia. In an era when, throughout Europe, small scale independent producers and retailers are losing market share to the dominance of multiple retail chains and industrialised agriculture, groups like the organic farmers and growers of west Wales are a vital element in the preservation of a continuing tradition.

South Tyrol

Although the Austro-Hungarian Empire has long ceased to exist, its legacy lingers on. In Northern Italy the old province of Tyrol extends 80 miles south of the border at the Brenner Pass, and Austrian German is still the first language for most of the population. In fact south Tyrol was ceded to Italy after the First World War and many Italians moved into the area and settled in the northern towns. Today some two thirds of the population are ethnic Germans. Between the wars the Fascist government attempted an Italianisation of south Tyrol and it was forbidden to teach German in schools and all the towns, villages, mountains and valleys were given Italian names. Now the area is bilingual, though in some of the high valleys a tenth of the population speak an old Ractian dialect, Ladin, partly derived from Latin.

The traditional character of the area is under threat as agriculture declines and tourism develops, but south Tyrol is still an important fruit growing region. In the cooler northern valleys the orchards are mainly of apples, and some of the fruit from organically cultivated orchards has been available in Britain. Moving further south from the Brenner Pass the orchards increasingly give way to vineyards and there are a wide variety of premium wines from this region. The combination of south facing slopes and a sunny climate with over 2,000 hours of sunshine per year make it ideal for viticulture.

One of the most popular wines is Kalterersee, which comes from the area just south of Bozen (Italian, Bolzano). I was first introduced to this wine by Barbara's uncle, Hansfried, whose artists brush making company Da Vinci, though based in Nuremberg, has a regional sales office or *Filiale* in Bozen. From the very first bottle I fell for this mellow red wine made from the *Vernatsche* grape (*Schiava* in Italian); it is a soft fruity wine, light in colour with a ripe cherry taste and a pleasant bitter after taste, and I vowed some day to visit the area.

This part of Italy is also important for its vegetables and salads, and when I finally made it to south Tyrol I walked through the streets of Bozen and marvelled at the market stalls piled high with local produce: grapes, tomatoes, courgettes, aubergines, mushrooms, endives, bunches of rocket, radiccio, and huge heads of Treviso chicory, while in the nearby arcades the delicatessen shops were packed cram full of cheeses, hams and salami. It was September and I'd travelled by train from Nuremberg to meet Hansfried and his wife, Marianne, in Bozen. The train stopped quite regularly after Munich, serving as a commuter train between Innsbruck, Brenner and Brizen before continuing on to Bozen and finally to Milan. Just before Innsbruck I went to the empty dining car and had lasagne and a cappuccino. I sat looking across the fertile valleys of Austria with fields of vegetables and maize overshadowed by high snow capped mountains behind which the evening sun was already slipping. Although it was late in the day, as the train started the long descent after the Brenner Pass, I could feel the warmth of Italy and the pull of the south.

Later in Bozen we went to a restaurant and had risotto with small cep mushrooms followed by fillet steak and then fresh raspberries and cream. Risotto is a north Italian classic and only in the north of the country is the rainfall high enough for rice to be grown. In September the ceps were in season and so were the autumn raspberries grown in the high valleys above Bozen. The next morning was scheduled for a walk in Seisser Alm, a high plateau bounded by the spectacular Rosen Garten, a semi-circle of jagged limestone peaks that glow pink in the setting sun . It was clear and warm with only occasional clouds, absolutely ideal for walking but we were all in a good sweat by the end. We finished up in a small mountain restaurant where we had *gluhwein* and *Kaiserschmarrn*; an Austrian speciality, it is a kind of sweet omelette served with a caramel coating. Frau Rottner, Barbara's mother, makes a similar dish called *Eierschmarrn* which is a traditional way of using up left over bread and rolls. These are crumbled up and left to soak in milk so that the bread becomes a *brei*, or porridge. The *brei* is then whisked up with eggs and cooked in hot butter or oil like an omelette. There's a savoury version when fried bacon and onion are added to the mixture, or a sweet version with sugar and jam like *Kaiserschmarrn*.

In the afternoon we travelled to the village of Girlan, south of Bozen, and I was finally in the centre of the Kalterersee Classico region. Here, adjacent to the wine cellars of Joseph Brigl, Da Vinci have their *filiale* and this was the tenth anniversary of its opening. There was to be a party for all the German and Italian staff, plus their sales representatives and major customers, so before everyone arrived we decked out the entrance with a garland of vine leaves hung with bunches of *Vernatsche* grapes. As we worked, tractors with trailer loads of grapes passed en route for the wine presses and throughout the area *federweisse* was available at the wine cellars. While all the others went for coffee I stood guard in case the garland should be vandalised, something that seemed most unlikely in such a quiet village. As I stood in the warm afternoon sunshine two village women came to inspect. One was ninety-two, and despite all my attempts to explain she remained convinced that we were about to open a new wine shop. She was obviously a strong nationalist and made it clear that the new shop should sell only Sud Tirol wines.

After the reception and some speeches we went by coach to a restaurant in a floodlit castle between Girlan and Bozen and here I enjoyed Kalterersee wine with typical local cuisine. To start there was wild boar ham with horseradish sauce and juniper berry butter, then a pasta course of tagliatelle with chanterelle mushrooms, mixed vegetables and small potato dumplings in sage butter. The meat course was stuffed guinea fowl and entrecôte steak with rice, potato croquettes and a salad of radicchio and endive. Finally the dessert was *krapfen alla tirolese*, a kind of local doughnut, but there were few from any of the nationalities present who could find room for it.

Going South

Greece

ALTHOUGH I had been twice to mainland Greece in the 1960s it wasn't until the early spring of 1975 that I went with my first wife to Crete. This was just an impromptu holiday, but I was already seriously thinking that it was time to leave London. Not that I was tired of the Great Wen, but rather I felt that I'd seen most things from an urban dweller's perspective and if I didn't change now perhaps that's all I would ever see. It wasn't a case of rejecting London life, rather an increasingly dominant urge to try something new, an unformed desire, and the idea of trying to make a living somewhere in the countryside by growing vegetables had certainly not yet crystallized. It is interesting now to look at the diary I kept and to see just how many entries are concerned with food and the cultivation of crops that we saw on our trip round the island. Also, a chance meeting in the south of the island with the farmer and naturalist David Thomas, from Cricieth in north Wales, seems in retrospect to have somehow foreshadowed our move to Cardiganshire. At the time he opened my eyes to many aspects of the Cretan countryside that I might otherwise have missed, and a couple of years later when we had moved to Ty'n yr Helyg I read that he had become a trustee of Bardsey Island, so the view out to sea became a constant reminder of the man and this influential trip to Crete.

Crete

I had been advised to travel west from Hiraklion. To the east lay the resorts developed for tourism, so we took the westward bound buses to Rethimnon, Chania, Tavronitis and Kastelli. Crete was occupied by the Venetians from 1212 to 1669; the Genoese occupied the island before them, and they were succeeded by the Ottoman Turks, but one of the most tangible legacies of the Venetian occupation are the harbours at Hiraklion, Rethimnon and Chania. The one at Chania is the most impressive, and on our first night we found it thronged with people stopping to eat and drink at the waterfront tavernas. Next day it was busy with all the activities of the fishermen. On the quayside a fisherman landed a huge tuna fish and a small crowd gathered to watch him gut it. We sat drinking ouzo and the waiter brought a plate of salami, octopus, cucumber, tiny bread rolls, and some flaky pastry with a filling of herbs and cheese for us to nibble while we watched and sipped.

Beside the harbour and the old Venetian quarter the other main attraction for me was the huge covered market. Built in the shape of a cross, it has north, south, east and west entrances. Where the arms of the cross intersect there was a kiosk selling newspapers and cigarettes. Inside, with its high ceiling, it seemed like a cathedral dedicated to food, with everything displayed magnificently on open stalls. The north and south arms were devoted to fruit and vegetables, olives and fresh herbs, cheeses, yogurts and milk. The east and west arms were primarily meat and fish: salami, dried fish, sheep carcass, skinned rabbit, pigs' heads, octopus, squid and a great shiny, slippery arrangement of freshly caught fish with, here and there, a small pot of flowers and herbs for decoration. Despite the spectacular fresh produce displays of the open air markets in Nuremberg, Bozen, and the country towns of France, I've seen nothing since to challenge the gory glory of those stalls in Chania, except perhaps the street markets of Naples. In fact it was only three years later that I was running a produce stall of my own in the tiny covered market in Aberystwyth. There can be no comparison. In Aberystwyth the market was restricted to a mere eight stalls, and with some misplaced notion of fairness, the Council permitted only one trader of each type in the hall, so mine was the only fruit and vegetable stall. The WI and a bakery shared the other fresh produce stand (but only opened on two days of the week), and the six remaining stalls changed with monotonous regularity. Gradually I expanded and introduced more lines to supplement the vegetables: plants and flowers, local butter and cream, yogurts, locally caught crabs and lobsters and eventually we built a considerable trade especially in home grown organic produce. But Chania it was not.

After Chania and Kastelli we took the route south to Paleohera. The bus went over the mountains along a narrow road with a succession of bends, through valleys and gorges past scattered farms and vineyards. There was a brief stop at the mountain village of Kandanos, then on again down to the southern coast at Paleohera, a small town on a peninsula, surrounded by superb coastal views to the east away in the direction of the Samarian Gorge, the mountain peaks were covered in snow. Like most Greek towns it seemed full of tavernas and barber's shops and, although it had only one hotel many local families let rooms. Some visitors were also camping amongst the trees by the beach and, out on the peninsula, some hard core hippies were living in caves.

By the hotel a small road, hardly more than a rough track, led to the mountain village of Anedri. Each night a bus brought the men of the village down to Paleohera, returning home much later when all the tavernas had closed. Walking this little road by day we passed a small estuary where some brightly painted boats had been pulled up from the rock-pebble shore line, and we walked on through some intensively farmed land. The agriculture seemed very mixed. Near to the town, where the land was level, there were some cows, and fields of vegetables: potatoes, tomatoes and cucumbers. Further along the road there were flocks of sheep amongst the orange groves, and higher up on the mountain slopes just olives and goats. On the advice of David Thomas, who was camping in the corner of a field near the town, we followed the road past the farms till we reached the second of two bridges. Here, to the right of the road, the hillside was fenced, but off through a wood and wire gate a winding trail led up to terraced fields and meadows high in the mountains. At first the trail followed a series of hairpins through shaded scrubby woodland with, here and there, clumps of wild gladioli, then it reached terraced mountain meadow land dotted with olive groves. Beneath the trees the meadows were carpeted with poppies and daisies, red and yellow amongst the spring green grass that stretched before us till it met the vivid blue of the Aegean sky. In the olive groves men were working, grafting new fruiting wood onto the old rootstocks. They pruned the trees hard and the new shoots were inserted into small slits in the end of the severed branches. The graft was covered with mud, or clay, then moulded into a ball with all the care of a potter forming a vase.

Finally we came upon the main reason for our climb, the orchids. The first we saw were butterfly orchids and then, farther on, bee orchids, and thereafter, along a high trail, we found a great number of both varieties, safe from the tethered goats that ate everything they could reach. The mountain sides rang with the song of sub-alpine warblers and, more visibly, the small grey, blue capped, white chinned, Sardinian warbler. As we followed a path back down the hillside towards the town the men finished their work and loaded up their donkeys, riding home on huge uncomfortable looking saddles made of canvas and great slats of timber.

In 1975 tourism was only just arriving in Paleohera and the first ice-cream refrigerator was about to be installed at the most 'progressive' bar when we left. Food and drink were still local and traditional. For breakfast we went to a house where a woman prepared fresh goat's yogurt with honey, and in the evening we walked into the kitchen of the popular local restaurant and peered into the pots and pans to see what was being cooked for supper. Here the most enjoyable meal was dolmades, vine leaves stuffed with rice in a sauce of tomatoes, oregano and olive oil. The soups were very filling, usually large bowls of lentils or chickpeas. The fish dishes varied widely. Freshly caught and fried the small fishes were excellent, but the dried fish that was cooked up and served with a stinking white sauce was disgusting and full of bones. Omelettes were excellent, but the meat, usually stringy, fatty mutton, was best avoided. Every meal was accompanied by bread, retsina and salads of tomato, cucumber and crisp red onions topped with feta cheese and an olive oil dressing.

On the plane home I met my first real olive oil enthusiast whose hand luggage comprised a newly pressed five litre bottle. My own prize purchase was a pair of knee length Cretan leather boots, but the images of food and farming from the island were to prove even stronger than the stout footwear I'd bought at a street stall in Chania.

The French connection

IN THE 1960s and 70s I was an obsessive francophile: at college, when my head should have been in sociology texts, I spent my evenings instead with Sartre and Simone de Beauvoir, with Camus, Saint-Exupéry, Genet and Gide. By the early 1970s friends had gone to live in Paris and I hungered to live there myself. Meantime, in London, I turned to Levi Strauss and Althusser, smoked Gitanes and argued existentialism and Marxism over bottles of Côtes du Rhône. When not arguing, or eating at bistros like Le Gourmet in Richmond, I played music with friends and after a few glasses of Pernod or Ricard it seemed I could play like the Bird himself – ah such is the power of pastis! By 1973 my obsession had become absolute. Wearing a Basque beret and *bleus de travail* I went every week to study in a language laboratory and wrote for jobs to the Centre d'études des mouvements sociaux in Paris, the Institut de sociologie in Toulouse and the UER de sociologie-ethnologie in Aix-en-Provence. But all to no avail.

Dordogne and Lot-et-Garonne

One early spring I went with my first wife and friends to look for *maisons abandonnées* in the Dordogne and Lot-et-Garonne. After nearly a decade in Cardiff and London I found a countryside I had forgotten existed, profuse in blossom and wild flowers. We stopped at country restaurants where vases of freshly picked cowslips adorned the table and ate salads of young dandelion leaves straight from the meadows. The hedgerows were full of nesting blackcaps and whitethroats, and the evening dusk was heavy with the scent of wallflowers. Two friends did eventually make the move and rented a cottage near Monpazier. Since both Gordon and Haley were artists, and Gordon had regular work as an illustrator, they were able to live where they pleased; and Moulin de la Seguine at Blanquefort-sur-Briolance became my second home. It was in a forest of chestnut trees, one of the many watermills in a small valley that until the 1950s and 1960s ground all the grain produced in the surrounding area, but by the 1970s, doors and shutters peeling, stood abandoned and empty. Moulin de la Seguine stood just past a *lavoir* and a tiny trout stream ran right under the mill with a beautifully clear spring 100 metres away. When we arrived in summer there were heavily laden fig and walnut trees on either side of the mill and if you walked behind the house there were meadows in a clearing on higher ground. Here the midday heat became intense with a tremendous cacophony from crickets and cicadas. As we walked up to the meadow from the mill the dry brown grass crackled and clouds of butterflies and grasshoppers flew up from underfoot. Below, the forest was at its most beautiful just after sunrise, the only cool time in a summer's day, when a pinkish mist drifted in amongst the trees and a million cobwebs were beaded with dew. Hoopoes flew about and jays called.

This area of south west France is famous for its insect life and entomologists come from all over Europe to study here. The insects also attract reptiles and during one stay a big green lizard with a blue chin fell into the hole that served as a lavatory; fortunately Gordon had just cleared it out and despite efforts to remove him the lizard chose to stay there. More alarmingly a large snake also took up residence in the lavatory so, at night, to scare the serpent away we took a large baton and beat frantically on the door, rather like announcing the start of a performance in a french theatre.

During our spring visits we ate round a large table in the mill with a log fire blazing in the hearth. There were large bowls of soup made from the last of the stored potatoes, and the first lettuces and asparagus from the garden. In summer the mill became overcrowded with visitors from Britain and we ate dishes of ratatouille and tomato salad outside on long tables lit by candlelight. Occasionally, especially in August, these meals under the stars would be terminated by another speciality of the region: sudden and violent thunderstorms. Back inside the mill we played poker and three card brag, or scared ourselves witless with a ouija board while thunder bolts burst overhead and lightning lit up the entire valley every few seconds.

The vegetable garden was just behind the mill and I loved to work there during our visits. The soil was rich and productive, the climate ideally suited for growing. After our first spring holiday Gordon wrote in June 1974 to invite us back for the summer, *"Tonight we ate the first batch of peas from the garden. We've got so many lettuces that we have to eat one a day to keep ahead. Everything else is doing fine. Tomatoes, courgettes, beetroots, carrots, cucumbers, radishes, spring onions, spinach, cabbage, beans. The field of potatoes that you planted looks luxuriant, like an organised jungle."*

On one memorable journey home we stopped in a village called Helles in Normandy and discovered the pleasure of cooked leeks served cold with a vinaigrette dressing. The next day after a final plate of *fruits de mer* on the quayside in Cherbourg I decided to continue the enjoyment of driving through the countryside by taking the minor roads from Southampton back to London instead of the M3. It was a sad and dismal experience and I vowed to leave London and south east England as soon as possible.

I remember the outstanding meals we had in the country restaurants of Lot-et-Garonne and Dordogne but somehow France and its culture is no longer the potent force it was. My disenchantment was slow, gradual and uneven. One summer on the way to Moulin de la Seguine we stopped to spend a night with a friend in rue Gabrielle in the Paris 18th Arrondissement. In the morning we found that the car had been broken into. Everything we had stupidly left in it had gone: a tape recorder and record player, money, food, a guitar and most painful for me, my saxophone. I still blame the premature demise of my musical career on the poor people of Paris.

Normandy

Some years later Barbara and I won second prize in a food competition organised by the magazine *Country Living*, and this brought a brief remission in the disillusionment with France. The prize was a short stay in Chateau de la Salle, near Coutance in Normandy. It was a classic country hotel with magnificent gardens, huge dining rooms, *nouvelle* cuisine and a tiled bedroom with a four poster bed. In the surrounding countryside, between the showers, the gentle April sun highlighted cider orchards where the black faced *vaches normandes* grazed under ancient apple trees just as, until the quite recent past, Hereford cattle grazed under standard apple trees along the Welsh borders. The apple trees have now been replaced with heavy cropping apple varieties on dwarf rootstocks, and the cattle moved to grass leys. Here in Normandy the woods were still coppiced for firewood and the hedgerows browsed by goats. Sows, hens and ducks wandered the meadows and there were small fields of carrots and leeks. Men with pitchforks spread steaming piles of manure, but as we ventured further afield we realised that this was a vestige of the rural France that is disappearing as surely as is peasant farming all over Europe.

Somehow by the 1980s and 1990s the magic of France and its allure for the British seemed to be replaced by Italy. Tuscany ousted Dordogne; pasta, sun-dried tomatoes and shoe-shaped loaves epitomised culinary trends. Italian opera, cars, women, Nessun Dorma and Pavarotti became the cultural symbols favoured by the media, and with Sartre all but forgotten, the post-modernist intellectuals turned to read an Italian, Umberto Eco.

Italy

Under the volcano

ALTHOUGH NORTHERN ITALY is important for wines and salad growing there is a different culinary tradition in the mezzo-giorno, the region south of Naples, and particularly in Sicily and the Aeolian Islands.

During my first visit I went as far south as it is possible to go, although the itinerary was actually accidental. Travelling in convoy down the Autoroute du Sud our companions on a motorcycle combination had a breakdown near Lyons. Leaving them to make some roadside repairs we agreed to meet at a camp-site near Marseilles, but failing that what should we do? We agreed on an ultimate rendezvous at the most southerly camp-site on our map, which turned out to be at Ragusa, the last town in Sicily before Africa. Despite heroic efforts with an ailing motorbike they didn't make it all the way and, out of money and out of luck, they were eventually repatriated from Naples by HM government.

Naples

Nearly twenty years later when we arrived at Naples airport on our way to Stromboli in the early summer of 1993, my companion Rick, whose mother is from Naples, said that compared to northern Italy the south is more like Africa. This seems to be a feeling shared by many travellers; for example when, in Jupiter's Travels, Ted Simon set off for his four year round the world motorbike trip, he headed south through Italy towards Sicily and Africa with growing excitement: *"To Naples and Salerno…I feel I am already leaving Europe, I can feel Africa there, so vast I am already within its aura"*

Similarly the more prosaic Economist Intelligence Unit gets carried away in similar mood in its report on Naples which they call: *"an emporium for the whole of the south…[which]…excites comparison with the third world."*

We arrived after dark, but already in early June the night time temperature was 24°C, and the moon was lighting up the bay. From our balcony at the waterfront Hotel Miramare we could see divers swimming out from the jetty to harpoon fish by torchlight; there were men fishing with rod and line from the sea wall, and along the harbour more people fishing with nets. We ate next door at La Cantinella, a restaurant naturally specialising in seafood where, according to the EIU, the impression fostered is that this is the haunt of the great and powerful. We drank Greco di Tufo Nouaser, a cool fruity white wine made from grapes grown high in the hills behind Naples, and over risotto with asparagus and *fruto di la mare*, we watched large parties of the 'great and powerful' at play till finally the restaurant closed and we all spilled out onto the pavement. Here some of the poorer and less powerful Neapolitans tried to persuade the men to buy fresh tulips for their women from the huge bunches they desperately thrust forward as the diners climbed into their Alfa Romeos and sped away.

We walked the seafront cafés and restaurants till 2am, yet the traffic and crowds never slackened. There had been two weddings and, prostrate on the sea-wall, a couple in full bridal costume were writhing and wrestling, their nuptial passion being captured on video for posterity. Further along, at Via Pompone de Algero under the great fortified walls of the old citadel of Castell dell'oro, and around the yachting marina, is the greatest concentration of open air bars and restaurants. Even in the small hours of the morning it was packed with diners, thronged with people strolling around, the lights making it as bright as day. Eventually, we retraced our steps to the hotel, just stopping for a last *grappa* at the American Bar Charlene and leaving the activity of Naples undiminished.

Next morning we stood on the aft deck of the *aliscafo* (hydrofoil) and sailed past Capri heading south west in perfect weather. Five hours later we were with the Orlandi at their restaurant Puntazzo in Ginostra.

I first met Renato Orlando when Rick was working at the University of Messina in Sicily. He was then a young economics lecturer and much involved in left wing politics and the Manifesto Party. Now, twenty years later, I met him again, but by this time he was no longer an economics lecturer, and I was no longer a sociology lecturer: he ran a bar-restaurant on the Island of Stromboli; I ran a farm and Salad Shop in west Wales. "Frost," he said, "I had a letter from you years ago; it said 'keep in touch', so I do", and he prodded me hard on the shoulder.

Stromboli

Stromboli is in the Aeolian archipelago north of Sicily. There are seven principal islands, the largest of which are Lipari, Vulcano, and Salina, in a group running north to south. To the west of these are Alicudi and Filicudi, to the north east Panerea and Stromboli. The whole of the archipelago is volcanic in origin.

Puntazzo, the bar-restaurant run by the Orlandi (Renato, together with his brother Riccardo and sister-in-law Loredano), is in Ginostra, a small village, a cluster of houses and terraces under the volcano at one extreme end of the island. There are no roads, no cars; everything goes up the steep winding path to the village by donkey. Stromboli is one of Europe's few remaining active volcanos and its name derives from the Greek, *strombos* meaning cone-shaped. As recently as 1930 a huge eruption catapulted giant pieces of rock out of the crater as far as Ginostra and a lava flow of 700°C reached the sea at San Bartolo, destroying vineyards and fig and olive groves. Since the island is cone shaped, and the active volcano has ash and lava screes running straight down its sides to the sea there are no routes from the village of Stromboli at one end connecting it to Ginostra at the other. In this respect the situation is identical to the one portrayed in

Roberto Rosselini's 1950 film 'Stromboli' which reaches a climax when the heroine played by Ingrid Bergman tries to escape from an unhappy marriage to a local fisherman by climbing the volcano in search of a route round the crater to Ginostra.

As there is no airport, the only way to reach the island is by sea, and there is a regular ferry boat and hydrofoil (or *aliscafo*) service between all the main islands linking them to Naples on the mainland and to Messina and Milazzo on Sicily. The principal company is SIREMAR – Sicilia Regionale Maritima. Because Ginostra has no deep water harbour, neither the ferry nor the Aliscafo can actually dock there, so whatever the weather, the only way ashore is by a transfer on the bobbing sea into a small dinghy; and so, from the outset, a visit has a sense of excitement, a *frisson* of danger. The village consists of houses scattered around the restaurant in a jumble of terraces, a dry river course, and groves of oranges, almonds and capers. Now only some 25 households live in Ginostra, and many of the houses are let in the summer time to tourists. There is little agriculture here although capers, once a major crop exported all over Europe, are still harvested. The caper, (Capperis spinosa) is a native Mediterranean herb and it grows wild by waysides and in rocky areas. In Ginostra it is cultivated in small groves around the village, and grows as a bush with greyish foliage and thorny stems. It has beautiful pale purple flowers, with stamens of a darker hue. The fruit picked by hand and pickled in a dry brine, is a powerful tonic according to herbalists, and in culinary use capers stimulate digestive juices and increase appetite. In the restaurant, Riccardo, *il coco*, uses capers extensively in sauces and salads, along with his other favourite herb, rocket, which he grows in the small garden near their house. The high heat of summer, plus the overall aridity of the climate, severely restricts the possibility of serious vegetable growing. Beside herbs they grow salads in the late winter and early spring, but as summer approaches the combination of a busy workload at the restaurant plus the heat and drought means that for most of the year they rely for vegetables on supplies from Sicily. The food at Puntazzo is classically Mediterranean, with lots of olive oil, garlic and herbs; vegetables like peppers, tomatoes and aubergines; pasta; fish (but comparatively little meat) and, of course, salads with every meal. Pasta with sweet peppers is a good illustration, served with spaghetti and sprinkled with a little grated Parmesan cheese. From the bar Renato recommends the Sicilian wine Cellaro Bianco with this dish.

The main traditional occupation for villagers is fishing, and the restaurant Puntazzo is named after a locally caught fish. Many of Riccardo's recipes are fish and pasta, like *ricciola* (amberjack) with tomato and caper sauce; spaghetti with a herb, caper and cuttlefish sauce; and *sciabola* (scabbard fish) cooked au gratin and served with a fresh tomato salad. The grilled and barbecued fish dishes are invariably served with a hot wine sauce. Although the meals are mainly of fish, on two evenings during our stay Riccardo made meat dishes, *polpette*, and *involtini alla messinese*. *Polpette* are little meat balls of minced beef, and they were served with *polpette di melanzane*, croquettes of aubergine made with garlic, basil and breadcrumbs, bound with egg and cooked in oil. *Involtini alla messinese* are very thin pieces of veal rolled up with a paste of breadcrumbs, olive oil and parsley and then dry fried.

The great favourite at Puntazzo is pizza. Riccardo is somehow reluctant to cook pizza, but when he does the word spreads round the village, maybe even round the islands, and the restaurant is packed. They're cooked in a wood fired oven, a beehive shaped construction of stone where the fire is built inside the oven itself. On our pizza evening Rick, Gerry and I cleared out the ashes and stacked wood next to the oven. In the evening Riccardo lit the fire, piling in the huge logs from local almond and olive trees. Later as the fire reduced to the glowing of the largest logs the oven was ready for use. Riccardo makes a yeast dough, rolling it out very thinly just as Barbara does when making apfel strudel. When he's made sufficient rounds he coats them with a tomato and oregano sauce, then adds chunks of the full fat cheese, *galbanino,* and covers them with extra virgin olive oil. The pizzas are then loaded into the hot oven on long flat scoops. In the fierce heat the dough rises quickly then crisps, the cheese, the oil and the tomato sauce all cook in no time and the result is a wonderful pizza of molten cheese, rich sauce and the thinnest, succulent, crisp pastry.

Lipari

The largest and most important island of the Aeolian group is Lipari and, like Stromboli, the main town has the same name as the island as a whole. The town surrounds a large extended harbour which is always busy with fishing boats and ferries coming and going. The island has roads and these seem jam packed with cars, vans, scooters and even high performance motorbikes. After a week in car-free Ginostra all this traffic seems completely unnecessary: the road mileage is very low, yet on the newly-built part of the harbour, finished lavishly in marble paving blocks, brand new taxis line up to ferry arrivals the short distance to their hotels. Naturally the harbour is lined with waterfront cafés where we sat drinking coffees and *granite sicilia*, crushed ice in a glass topped with coffee or strawberry then lots of cream (there's also a lemon version without cream). It is usually accompanied by a *brioche*; you break pieces off the sweet roll and dip them in the *granite*.

The town was intensely hot during our visit, but the streets are very narrow and the buildings extremely tall so there is a great deal of shade, and our hotel, Enzo il Negro, was exceedingly cool with an en-suite shower and big windows shuttered against the midday sun. Above the harbour, high on a cliff and dominating the town, stands the old citadel dating from the fourth century. First Roman, then Saracen, then Norman, the citadel was besieged in 1544 by the Ottoman Turks when 140 ships lay off the island. The siege lasted ten years and the town was finally sacked. The citadel now houses a museum of archaeology, a youth hostel, three churches and a cathedral.

Lipari has a famous restaurant, the Filippino, founded in 1910. It is a large place, wonderfully situated in Piazza Mazzini o Municipio, a leafy square above the harbour. We found the food and service good, but not memorable. The pasta courses were very filling, the main fish courses unexciting. Gerry dropped a fork and a waiter swooped to change it immediately; as it was out of season the restaurant was not busy and seemed over staffed but as we ate the tables gradually filled up. Well-dressed men, elegant women, stunning young women in the tiniest clinging black micro dresses: the groups looked as if they had just come from a Roman fashion house. But compared with Riccardo's work at Puntazzo the food at Filippino seemed institutional. In Ginostra the Orlando brothers have created something special; the bar is Renato's theatre and the restaurant is very simple with tables on the terraces, candlelit at night, and the kitchen screened off by bamboo curtains. Behind these Riccardo cooks like the undiscovered artist, striving to achieve a standard he believes in, creating meals as much for himself as for the customers whom he feels only rarely appreciate the quality. In fact recognition is coming, Puntazzo is now included in the same restaurant guide as Filippino, and as praise for the new entry increases, the reports on the older one become more muted.

On the day we were due to leave Stromboli there was a mighty swell and the sea was running behind a strong wind from the north; in fact the *aliscafo* didn't even bother to come to Ginostra. The sea was dark blue with high, white-crested waves and the air was so clear that Sicily was just visible for the first time on the horizon. Condemned to stay another day at least we helped our hosts by putting a rush mat shade roof on the lower terrace, expanding the bar-eating area ready for the high summer tourist invasion. Somehow, working in just shorts under the hot sun led to numerous jokes about building the bridge over the River Kwai. Later we showered as usual and changed for dinner in almost colonial fashion. The trick, as always, lay in having pumped up the water from the well into the tank on the roof in the morning. By the evening the sun had warmed the tank and the water for the shower was hot. After dinner I felt very tired and left the restaurant early to go to bed. Our room, the 'cube' over Renato's house, reminded me of nothing more than the punishment cell in the Kwai film. After the day long sun it had got very hot and Gerry and Rick's attempt to keep out midges and mosquitoes made it worse. Their *spiralette* filled the room with foul smoke and the closed windows and door left it stifling. When they eventually returned I had to get up and we sat on the veranda drinking brandy. Behind us the plume from the volcano was regularly coloured pale red from small eruptions and above us was the infinity of the Milky Way, a shooting star, a satellite and a dark cloud floating over the sea. Ginostra village was very dark since there is no electricity, but across the straits the lights of Panerea and Lipari shone all night long. Although we knew we would soon be leaving, as we sat round our last candle with our backs to the volcano, cut off from the rest of the world by the force of the sea, we felt the full magic of the place.

Going West

The Canary Islands

ALTHOUGH OUR visits to Gasthaus Rottner are generally times of great celebration like weddings, birthdays and christenings, many of the Rottner family are often preoccupied with the daily demands of restaurant work and their other jobs. Similarly when family Rottner come to Ty'n yr Helyg we have often been much involved with the work demands of farm and business. The full answer is the joint holiday, both families away from home on some neutral territory. Since the quietest time of the year for all of us tends to be in January we've sought out sunny islands which are warm even in mid-winter, and twice we've ended up in the Canaries on the islands of El Hierro and La Palma. These two, together with La Gomera, are the smallest islands in the archipelago and lie to the west of

Tenerife. The climate is warm and springlike throughout the year and the Canaries are important exporters of bananas, early potatoes, tomatoes, peppers, cucumbers and avocados to Britain and the rest of Europe. Traditionally Canary tomatoes filled the winter gap between the end of the mainland Spanish season and the start of the Channel Island and home produced crop in the spring. In recent years, although the Guernsey Island producers have been virtually forced out of business by high transport costs and poor returns, the development of the glasshouse industry both in the UK and in the Netherlands has put a great deal of pressure on the Canary exporters. The great advantage of the Canary tomato crop is its flavour. Naturally ripened by the sun and traditionally grown outdoors, the fruit has well balanced sweetness and acidity compared with the poor taste and watery texture of the forced, out-of-season glasshouse crop grown in northern Europe. Fortunately there is an expanding organic tomato business in the Canaries and there are some 300 acres of organic tomatoes grown there, mostly around Playa del Inglés on Gran Canaria. Many of these are exported directly to Wales to supply the British market, or to the Netherlands.

El Hierro

El Hierro has no international airport, so to get there it is first necessary to fly to Reina Sofia airport in Tenerife, and then to take a bus or taxi to the northern airport, which is between Puerto de la Cruz and the capital Santa Cruz de Tenerife. From here it is a short flight in a 40 seater - twin engined Fokker Friendship to Hierro's airport on the coast, near the capital Valverde.

We arrived in Tenerife on New Year's Day in 1988, which was really a mistake. Not only was everywhere packed with other holiday makers, but also there were no buses. Outside the airport the taxi drivers were only interested in ferrying tourists to their villas and hotels, and for quite a while none of them wanted to know about the party of two adults and five children who were trying to get to Puerto de la Cruz. In the end two of the more entrepreneurial drivers decided that they could take us in two taxis at a cost of 14,000 pesetas. (On our return journey two weeks later the southward bound trip in one Peugot 504 cost only 500 pesetas).

In the south of Tenerife, which is the region most developed for tourism, the scenery is arid and barren but even here some tomatoes and bananas are grown. The plots are in ravines by the coast and usually surrounded by palisades of wooden fencing as a windbreak; there's a large variety and range of polytunnels here too. Along the entire route there is sea-front development, and in the south the huge advertisement hoardings on the barren hillsides are hideously like the billboards in the desert states of the USA. As the road climbs upward along the coast to the capital Santa Cruz the scenery becomes greener with more cultivation. The capital is comparatively large and industrial for the Canaries, but Puerto de la Cruz, where we eventually stayed for the night before catching the plane to Hierro, was rather verdant, surrounded by banana plantations with botanical gardens nearby, and everywhere flowers in bloom and huge bushes of poinsettias.

El Hierro took us by surprise. We were out for a simple winter break in the sun, but the island's charm, its isolation and mystery were captivating. On such a small area, some 109 square miles, there are complete scenic contrasts. The south is arid , the north greener, and, in between, the central upland area is patterned with small stonewalled enclosures and pine forests, almost like parts of Wales. The whole island is in fact half of a volcano, the other half having fallen into the sea, leaving a huge gulf, El Golfo, on the north western side. Although there is no written ancient history of El Hierro there are some undeciphered rock engravings which pre-date Egyptian hieroglyphics at El Julán and La Caleta, and according to local legend the missing half was the lost city of Atlantis. The road from the capital Valverde comes over the lip of the crater and descends into El Gofio, down to the villages of Frontera and Tigaday. The steep cliffs are breathtaking and the remote green screes that tumble down from the sheer drop known as El Risco into the sea are one of the last habitats for Lacerta simonyi, the giant lizard that grows a metre and a half long.

The bay around Frontera is the most cultivated part of the island. Once it was nearly all grapes, but now there are papayas, pineapples, avocados and, of course, potatoes and bananas. The soil is black and volcanic, the plots mostly small terraces around the stone built homesteads. Nearest to the sea, on the flattest land where the sun comes earliest each day, there are large commercial holdings and a great block of polytunnels. Looking out to sea from our accommodation near Tigaday we could occasionally see the ghostly form of La Palma appearing through the evening mist at sunset. It looked close, but in fact it is 100 miles to the north.

The sea port is at La Restinga which is south from El Golfo, and we reached it by hired car through the central pine forest area and the Parque del Morcillo. After the pine woods there is a pastoral area of terraced hillsides with orchards of almond trees, which, in January, were in full pink blossom. Further south the scenery becomes more arid and here there were flocks of goats and the odd sheep. Lower down still the hillsides are bare rope lava flows and it looks as if the flows solidified only yesterday. La Restinga has a sea wall and a small harbour where the cargo and fishing boats come in, but it seemed a rather scruffy sort of place and we didn't stay long. On the way home to Tigaday we bought freshly caught sea bass and red mullet and took them home to eat with boiled potatoes, crusty bread and tomato salad; a delicious foretaste of another meal yet to come.

In the extreme west of El Hierro there is a lighthouse at Playa de Orchilla, and until 1492 this was the end of the world. One hundred and fifty years later the Duc de Richelieu adopted Punta Orchilla, just beyond the lighthouse, as the official meridian, and according to the travel writer Henry Myhill: *"the last and entirely appropriate supporter of this meridian, right up to 1918, was the Austro-Hungarian Empire."*

Here, between the lighthouse and the black sand beach at Playa el Verodal, is where the sabinar tree grows and many specimens are contorted into curious shapes by the strong winds blowing onto El Hierro from the great expanse of the Atlantic Ocean. One of these trees is so bent that its trunk is growing parallel to the ground, and the Herranos have adopted it as their emblem. Further curiosities of this tree are that it has no real bark, and its seed will only germinate after passing through the gut of a raven. This fact, often unknown to visitors, has defeated many attempts to propagate the seed when it has been taken off the island, but it is a symbiotic relationship that exists between many plants and animals. As Harold McGee writes: *"[seeds] may be constructed so that they pass through an animal's digestive tract uninjured, and finish up in a freshly manured location. The wild tomato of the Galapagos Islands has developed a seed coat so tough that it requires the good offices of the tortoise to digest it away and make germination possible."*

We joined a fishing party by the stone jetty near the lighthouse, and Barbara's brothers went out in the dinghy with harpoons and came back with a marvellous variety of fish including tuna, sea bass, red mullet and parrot fish. With our guides we made a fire of driftwood on the beach and cooked the fish and ate them with *papas arrugadas*, potatoes boiled in sea water, and salad. We drank local *vino de Mesa* and bathed in the heaving swell of the ocean. The sun was very hot, and when it was my turn to go out in the dinghy to catch more fish to take home I was completely overcome by seasickness, and felt like death at the end of the world.

In contrast to the arid west of El Hierro, the region in the north east is productive dairy farmland. It is high above sea level and around San Andrés although it can be stormy in winter it can also be stifling hot in summer. There are extensive orchards here of apples, almonds and plums and the island's milk cooperative has its creamery at San Andrés where they make cheeses from both goat's and cow's milk. Barbara and I drove across the high plateau towards the clifftops one evening when the farmers were going into the fields with churns to hand milk the cows and goats. We turned off the road to Frontera and made a detour to Mirador de la Pena. Here the Lanzarote architect, César Manrique, has built a restaurant on a vertiginous rocky outcrop with a commanding view overlooking El Gofio. Unfortunately for us the restaurant was not open. We did eat out however, and at our first meal in a local bar in Frontera I ordered black eyed beans and fried bananas. Barbara had a couscous vegetable dish cooked in banana leaves, the other members of our large party had steak, rabbit, kid or squid, and the children had macaroni. This was very much a locals' place to eat, whereas down at the old harbour there are the first restaurants catering for the incipient tourist trade. The one with the highest reputation in 1988 was Restaurant Noemi at Las Puntas run by an Italian woman called Gemma Chinosi where we had an excellent meal the night we celebrated the 22nd birthday of Barbara's brother Hannes. The restaurant specialized in seafood and had an excellent reputation for its fresh fish. When we went to book a table Gemma was at first not keen to oblige because that very night she had arranged to fly to Tenerife. However her staff were happy to take care of the preparations and Gemma went off leaving them full instructions for the meal. We started with the typical small pointed loaves of fresh bread served with mayonnaise and tomato and pepper dips, or *mojo*. Then came fish soup followed by the main course of fried parrot fish, boiled potatoes and salad. We finished off with chocolate mousse, ice cream, coffee and Spanish brandy. Although the food was well cooked there was a peculiar wrong note – the potatoes, which Lawrence D Hills calls the 'good listeners' because they mingle discreetly with the other ingredients, were shouting out loud. In fact they tasted distinctly soapy, as if the plates still had washing up liquid on them. We conferred, and decided that the cooks had put parsley on the fish and coriander on the potatoes, an easy mistake but only a real coriander lover likes this herb on potatoes.

Although the paraphernalia of modernity is slowly coming to Hierro, where the first electricity was introduced only in 1974, the pattern of change is affected by newcomers. These fall into two categories. The first group aren't so much newcomers as returning expatriates: traditionally the young men of El Hierro went to Cuba in search of work, but after Castro's revolution in 1959 they went to Venezuela instead. By the late 1980s Venezuela was in recession and many Herranos were returning home with their savings and investing in new building developments and horticultural enterprises. The second group are the cultural refugees who have fled from the high tech pressures of urban Europe, or from the over commercialized and tourist saturated islands elsewhere in the Canaries. This heterogeneous group (and there are others like them in all the distant corners of Europe including west Wales) seek the traditions of El Hierro, its self sufficiency, its isolation from authority and bureaucracy, its remote beauty, and the friendliness and generosity of its people.

La Palma

In many ways El Hierro and La Palma are very similar, but La Palma is larger, with a surface area of 280 square miles, and at 76,000 its population is ten times greater than El Hierro's. In the larger island tourism is much more developed and it is a very popular winter holiday destination with weekly charter flights from Germany. There are the usual well established bars, restaurants, hotel and villa complexes. If there has to be a mass impact of one national group on the island then there is a good reason why it should be the eco-concerned Germans. As we've noticed with our visitors at home at Ty'n yr Helyg, they're very worried about pollution and go to great lengths to sort out their domestic refuse for re-cycling. On La Palma, as elsewhere, they demand non-polluting washing up liquids and soaps, and they avoid plastic containers and re-use glass jars whenever possible. So in Los Llanos the supermarkets have a better range of green cleaning fluids than in most UK towns, and at nearby El Paso there's a shop selling a wide range of wholefoods, wholemeal and homebaked bread, yogurt that you can buy in re-usable glass jars, local cheeses, and a range of organically grown fruit and vegetables. Several German families have settled on the island, with one growing oyster mushrooms, and another whom we visited having an organic avocado plantation. The reports are that on La Gomera this 'alternative' development has gone much further, to the extent that its now known as 'the muesli island'.

On the eastern coast of La Palma, near the airport at Mazo, there is a fresh produce market which is open two days a week. It comprises a large market hall with stalls which during our January visit in 1992, were selling locally grown carrots and potatoes, spring cabbage, capsicums, sweet potatoes, apples, oranges, mangoes, bananas, guavas, grapefruit and herbs. A few stalls sold homemade preserves and marmalades and outside a van drew up selling langustinos and fresh sea fish; but the market is no longer typical as bananas come increasingly to dominate La Palma's agriculture. There are now plantations throughout the island, except in the mountain areas, and huge plastic growing-houses for protected banana cropping near the sea on the hotter, dryer, western coast. From the newly erected packhouses lorry loads of bananas are continually despatched on the first leg of their journey to mainland Europe.

Whereas El Hierro is the remaining half of an extinct volcano, there is still volcanic activity on La Palma especially on the southern headland of Fuencaliente. We walked around the largest crater at Volcan de San Antonio which last erupted in 1677, an eruption lasting for 66 days. However there have been three more recent eruptions: El Chaco in 1710, San Juan in 1949, and the most recent at Teneguia in 1971 which lasted for 25 days. By the time of our visit in 1992 the crater at Volcan de Teneguia was quiet, but hot gases still escaped from fissures in the rock, the solidified lava was scorching to the touch, and the air smelt harsh and sulphurous. All along La Ruta de los Volcanos the landscape is bizarre, an undulating inhospitable terrain of volcanic ash; yet right up to the immediate slopes of the craters there are vineyards with prostrate vines growing in the black soil that looks just like clinker from the Rayburn. Under the sun, with no other vegetation for shade, it seems a cruel place to have to work, yet at least once a year the vines require pruning and harvesting.

In fact the Fuencaliente area around the Volcan de San Antonio is the main centre of Malvasian wine production. This is the Canary sack wine, much loved by Shakespeare's characters, especially Falstaff. It became famous throughout Europe from the 16th century onwards and was regularly imported into west Wales via Carmarthen at about this time. Grapes were one of the three great crops of the Canary Islands before the predominance of 20th century bananas and tomatoes; the others being sugar and cochineal. Many of the vine stocks in La Palma are now virtually unique since they escaped the infestation of Phylloxera vastatrix, an insect pest that bores into the roots of grape vines and kills them. Between the 1860s and the 1880s the pest spread through mainland European vineyards after it had been brought to Europe from North America on some native American vines. The European stocks had no resistance and the vineyards were devastated, but the pest didn't cross the seas to infect the Canary vines. The Malvasian vines grown near Fuencaliente are believed to be authentic stocks from the original vines introduced from the Greek island of Candia in the 15th century. They certainly reminded me of the Santorini wines I had drunk in Crete, again from vines grown in volcanic soil. We stopped at a roadside wine cellar and sampled Malvasian wine, two other white wines, a red and a rosé, all marketed under the Teneguia label. To most modern palates Malvasia seems very sweet, almost like a sherry and Konrad, Barbara's father and wine expert, pronounced it an apéritif wine.

From Fuencaliente we took a winding road down the mountains through banana plantations, irrigated from huge concrete reservoirs, until we came to a rough *pista* that took us to a small beach called Playa del Largo. This was like a smugglers' cove, the beach surrounded on both sides by rocks and a marvellously scenic collection of homemade beach huts. It was very much a locals' resort and looked somehow like a cross between a film set from 1930s Florida and the beach scene in Fellini's Amacord; quite unlike the tourist's favourite beach at Puerto Naos. In the middle of the cove there was an open-air bar-restaurant with a wooden terrace shaded by a canopy of sun bleached banana leaves. We ate salads and grilled fish whilst some of the more energetic of our group went snorkelling in the clear waters over the rocky shore line. I sat with my beer pondering the name Playa Del Largo and thinking of the movie Key Largo. Across the track from the bar a diesel generator thumped away and as I looked up from the table I half expected to see Humphrey Bogart walk around the corner.

Farther north in the Los Llanos area where we stayed, the most popular places to eat are the waterfront restaurants and, on the night of the Epiphany celebrations in the town, we started our evening with an all seafood meal of prawns, tuna fish, mussels and an odd sort of fish cake served like a lollipop on the end of a small lobster claw. There was plenty of Teneguia *bianca*, bread, salad, *papas arrugadas*, and the green and red *mojo* sauces. The meal terminated with a typical 'Rottner Hectic', as our party of 18 swept out of the restaurant into our four small Opel hire cars and rushed back to the town centre to see the start of the Epiphany procession. Mary, Joseph and the crib were on one float, and the Three Kings on another as the procession was towed towards the main square. Here a brass band played and children in costume waved palm fronds and threw sweets to the crowd. Later they paraded the packed streets with hand–held fireworks and we regrouped at a street café for a last brandy and to count that we had the right number of our own children to take back to the villa at La Palma Jardín.

We had two other notable meals in La Palma. The first was at Restaurant San Petronio at Lomo de las Animas, which is run by an unlikely named Italian family, Emilio and Gabriella Vanoostende together with their son and two daughters. The specialities here are fresh pasta and the desserts, which are cakes flavoured with zablioni, caramel, chocolate, coffee and pineapple, all made by Gabriella.

The second meal was back in Los Llanos and we arranged it to celebrate

Hannes' 26th birthday. In the end the evening was a success but this was mostly thanks to Cardinal Mendosa. On arrival we had apéritifs of sangría with small portions of smoked salmon, pâté and fish roes. This was followed by plates of mussels with shrimps, pipe fish and oysters. Next, the most successful course, was langustinos. After this Stefan announced that these appetizers had all been very well, but now he would really like something to eat. He had a long wait because it was a good half hour before the next dishes came. I had a plate of mixed deep fried fish, but just about everyone else had sole, and this was a complete disaster. The fish was far from fresh, and it was served with an unpleasant oily tomato sauce, microwaved potatoes that arrived on the plate in allu-foil, and some very badly cooked vegetables which Barbara described as "an unfortunate choice". This adoption of classic English understatement sent Stefan into peals of bitter laughter. Stefan was in merciless mood and felt that the chef should be sacked at the very least, but preferably shot. The hour was getting late so we skipped the dessert and finished with small cups of black coffee half filled with brandy. As a goodwill gesture the headwaiter also sent over a further round of complimentary brandies and so a more jocular mood began to replace the gloom that had arrived with the main course. Then it was back to La Palma Jardín for several more glasses of Cardinal Mendosa, the evening's saviour: smooth and slightly sweet, the premier Spanish brandy.

Postscript

RECENTLY, ONE December afternoon, I found myself in Cardiff with three hours to kill before the northbound bus left the Central station for Llanrhystud. It was a fine, bright day, cold but sunny, the city bustling with Christmas shoppers. I walked the city streets revisiting the haunts of my student days, checking out how much had changed in the intervening 25 years. I went to Cathays Park and then up to what had been the Arts Building, which seemed to house the Law Department. The old Dumfries Place had completely disappeared, together with the 'new' Students' Union. I strolled up St Mary's Street, along by the Castle, into Sophia Gardens and along the banks of the Taff. Back in the centre I found the Oriel Gallery and the bookshops in the Hayes. I walked through the covered market and the shopping arcades and finally chose somewhere to eat. Cardiff seemed greatly improved by the pedestrianization of Queen Street, but many of the murkier old corners where we used to go to clubs like the New Moon to see the New Welsh Jazz Orchestra have all gone, whereas the choice of places to eat seems to have increased a hundred fold. In the sixties we would alternate between the Students' Union, the Khardomah on Queen Street and the Woodville, the nearest pub to the Art's Building. Now in the shopping plazas whole floors are given over to numerous little restaurants and cafés and throughout the pedestrianized area there are salad bars, pizzerias, coffee bars and Italian restaurants; but as I walked the streets for several hours I couldn't help but notice that the most popular, the busiest, and the most consistently crowded were Macdonalds and Burger King.

Trends in eating are clearly moving in a number of very different directions. On the one hand, as the traditional pattern of family breakfast, lunch and roast dinner disappears, fast food, 'snacking' and 'grazing' are in the ascendancy despite the popularity of celebrity chefs. This too often means a diet of highly processed and adulterated food, bland in taste and sadly lacking in fresh ingredients. There's a great deal of evidence from food researchers that demonstrates this, but it is also there at the supermarket check-out: trolleys full of canned and frozen food, instant meals, microwave dinners. Too often it is also there in the High Street gutters in the morning, where discarded polystyrene cartons litter the streets with the uneaten remains of burgers and spare ribs, chips, curries, kebabs and fried chicken.

But it isn't all bad news. My work and travels have shown that from the hills and valleys of west Wales to many distant corners of Europe there is a continuing commitment to the idea that fresh food tastes best and is the most nutritious, that food is best eaten with the minimum of processing and as soon after harvest as possible, and that food is best produced organically from a healthy living soil without the use of artificial fertilisers, pesticides and fungicides. It is on these simple principles that our ideas on food and diet, and the recipes in the final chapter, are based.

CHAPTER 3

Food for thought

"Some people have a foolish way of not minding, or pretending not to mind what they eat. For my mind, I mind my belly very studiously, and very carefully; for I look upon it that he who does not mind his belly, will hardly mind anything else."

Dr Johnson

WHAT WE EAT, and its relationship to our health, has now become a major national concern, and it seems that for some of the more extreme commentators the whole of life has become a sort of illness that can only be cured by diet.

Eating in Britain

THE 1992 GOVERNMENT White Paper, *The Health of the Nation*, gave official approval to a general view amongst nutritionists that the nation's diet includes too much cholesterol and saturated fats, with high consumption rates of refined carbohydrates, salt, full fat dairy products and red meat, too little fruit and vegetables, whole grains, dietary fibre and low fat dairy products.

What has become strikingly apparent is that although killer diseases like smallpox and diphtheria have been virtually eradicated, and others like pneumonia and tuberculosis have become treatable, other diseases have taken their place, especially cancers, bowel disorders, coronary disease and diabetes. As Dr Hugh Sinclair pointed out, medical advances have greatly reduced the incidence of infant mortality, so more children survive into adulthood, but there has been little impact on the survival rates of people after middle age. In 1841 a

50 year old man might live on average a further 20 years, today the average is 23 years, a negligible advance.

Pioneering scientists like Hugh Sinclair and Sir Robert McCarrison sought to show that nutrition is basic to health, and although the importance of other factors (like stress and environmental pollution) cannot be overlooked, the link between diet and health in the so-called 'western diseases' is now increasingly accepted.

The role of the antioxidant vitamins beta carotene (which forms vitamin A in the body), and C and E are particularly important in reducing the risk of illnesses such as stroke, cancer and heart disease. Recent research at the Rayne Institute at London's St Thomas's Hospital has demonstrated, for example, the vital role of vitamins C and E in the prevention of heart and lung disease. The director of the heart research unit, Professor David Hearse told the *Grower* magazine, *"there is scope for boosting the body's natural vitamin C and E reserves and by doing this we can reduce heart and lung injury."* However, according to the Institute's nutritional biochemist, Dr Frank Kelly, the average British diet includes only 7 oz of fresh fruit and vegetables per day, whereas we should consume two or three times that amount. As Dr Kelly points out, *" lots of people recognize that vitamins are important and take tablets to compensate for them...but we are concerned that vitamins may not be absorbed and there are many other factors in fruit and vegetables, such as fibre, that may contribute to their uptake."* Most fresh fruit and vegetables contain vitamin C, particularly cabbage, brussels sprouts, potatoes, and radishes, whilst asparagus, spinach, carrots and tomatoes are good sources of vitamin E, and spinach, carrots, apricots, broccoli, and tomatoes contain betacarotenes. In all cases organically grown fruit and vegetables, eaten raw, are the best source of vitamins.

In the UK and Western Europe one group whose diet has moved closest to the approved dietary goals of the *The Health of the Nation* are those who regularly eat organic food. Researchers from the Food Policy Research Unit at the University of Bradford found that compared to the average British diet, these 'organic eaters' consumed more yogurt, more fresh fruit and vegetables (particularly more raw vegetables), and more wholefoods. Overall their diet showed a greater intake of fibrous foods and less consumption of animal foods, sweet foods and fatty foods than the rest of the population.

Although there is a great deal of evidence from surveys that consumers would like to eat more organic food, it is maintained that they are put off from buying more because of high prices and lack of availability. Price and availability are far from the whole story however, and in fact it has been shown that when people change to buying organic food they tend to rely less heavily on meat, processed foods and 'luxury' items with the result that the weekly shopping basket can actually be cheaper than for conventional food consumers. As a retailer I frequently felt irritated by those people who objected to organically produced food on the grounds that it was more expensive when, in fact, local prices of in-season organically grown vegetables were usually quite competitive. It seems that many people are prepared to buy exotic and out-of-season fruit and vegetables whilst complaining that they can't afford organic produce. Many restaurant chefs and people giving dinner parties at home, for example, often seem quite prepared to fork out large sums of money for mangetout peas from Guatemala, fine beans from Kenya, baby corn from Thailand, mangoes from Brazil, and out of season strawberries and raspberries from America and Chile in preference to local organic seasonal produce. The high price of these foods is not due their superior taste and quality but to their relative scarcity and expensive transport costs from production areas half a world away. The fact is that people don't buy on price alone, though of course for many people it is a major consideration. Economists call food an 'inferior good' by which they mean that as income rises so a smaller proportion is spent on food. Simply put, this means that poor people have to spend much more of their money on food than rich people do. The well off can buy prestige foods that confer status onto the purchaser, but unfortunately local organically grown vegetables, although a healthy option, just don't have the status of expensive imported exotics. I've seen many such customers spend large sums of money on very small quantities of expensive food for one meal; but I've also seen people on very low, often fixed, incomes spend much less and yet fill up two or more shopping bags with in-season local organic produce enough to feed their households for a week.

Although the surveys that show a latent demand for organic food are good news for the organic food lobby, they have to be read with some caution. Market researchers know that when it comes to answering awkward questions, particularly those about health, people give the answers they imagine the interviewers want to hear. Everyone wants to eat and live healthily, but for many comfort and convenience often come before the gains they might get from the change to more exercise and a healthier diet. Throughout the 1980s, according to the Fresh Fruit and Vegetable Information Bureau, convenience was the main factor affecting expenditure on fresh produce. Consumers increasingly bought food that was perceived as being convenient, so traditional vegetables like brussels sprouts and root crops suffered; and despite the scientific evidence that diets rich in green leafy vegetables are healthier, the consumption of green vegetables nearly halved between 1981 and 1991. Even consumption of potatoes fell as people turned to more easily prepared alternatives like rice and pasta. The only bright spot in their review was the growth in popularity of salads, which they found to have been particularly stimulated by packs of pre-washed and mixed salad leaves. If convenience is one of the major factors influencing food choice, the importance of salads can hardly be overstated.

The conclusions are clear. Salads and organic food can make a very significant contribution to an improvement in the nation's diet, but unfortunately this has yet to be taken on board by the establishment. To date organic food production has minimal grant aid or subsidy from the government despite its lack of availability. When, with colleagues from the University of Wales, Aberystwyth and the University of Reading I put up a research programme to investigate the processes involved in the growth of organic food consumption, the Economic and Social Research Council, who are funding a programme of research into the Nation's Diet, turned it down with the comment, *"The Committee felt that this was an interesting proposal but ultimately was unable to give it a high priority..."* What more can be said?

Diet and health

OBESITY IS now a major health problem in the affluent industrialised countries and one that is increasingly affecting children. The problem has a lot to do with sedentary life-styles and lack of exercise but is certainly exacerbated by eating habits. Researchers argue that many of the children who are overweight at age 11 will be overweight at the age of twenty six, and that the effects of obesity on health need to be tackled at an early age. Sadly there is plenty of evidence that children's eating habits don't follow national recommended guidelines. In a survey for TV's Channel 4 in 1993 it was found that over half the children ate no fruit or vegetables at all, but they ate lots of chips, snacks and sweets.

Subsequent reports serve to confirm these findings and they echo the disturbing diets recorded in the food diaries that Geoffrey Cannon presents in his book *The Politics of Food*. No doubt urban children are experiencing the divorce that is occurring between food production and consumption. As food gets more highly processed and packaged its relationship to farming and the land becomes increasingly obscure to many consumers. For several years Barbara's brother Hubert provided countryside holidays on his small farm in Franconia for deprived children from inner city Berlin. While they thoroughly enjoyed the countryside and the forests, the kids could be quite ambivalent about farming. In a classic case one boy refused any longer to eat eggs when he had seen one actually emerge from the rear orifice of a hen. He thought it was disgusting.

However, even in a rural farming area like west Wales there can be surprising barriers to the promotion of a healthy diet for school children. Our farm is right next door to a primary school and local people recall how in the past the farm supplied the kitchen with vegetables for school dinners. We tried to resurrect this relationship in the 1980s when we were producing a wide range of organically grown crops, but we were thwarted by the Council's policy of central buying which basically meant that the supply of fruit and vegetables was put out to tender for the whole of the education area, with no possibility for individual schools to buy their own local supplies. As our own children were eating dinners at school we felt it a contradiction that, while we grew organic produce a matter of yards from the school kitchen, our children had to eat chemically grown produce imported from England and elsewhere. In desperation we suggested that we could donate potatoes and other staples to the school free of charge, but this suggestion was also declined on the grounds that it would cause accounting difficulties and probably a loss of budget for the education authority.

On the other hand, and in complete ironic contrast, secondary schools in the area were following the national trend by installing vending machines supplied by a national company so that the children could buy chocolate, snacks and soft drinks during the school day. The schools achieve a short term goal of raising their revenues, but at the expense of the children's present eating habits and long term health.

As the report *Food for Children*, published in 1994, pointed out, there are no minimum standards for school meals. As one in nine school-age children eat no breakfast, and one in six do not have a cooked evening meal, many of them rely on snacks for energy throughout the day. The authors of the *Food for Children* report, the National Forum for Coronary Heart Disease Prevention, concluded that children's eating habits were a considerable cause for concern, high in fat and high in sugar, a combination that could lead to heart problems in later life.

Dieting

THE REASONS why we eat what we eat are complicated and are as much to do with fashion and cultural trends as they are to do with what we need to eat for nutrition or what we can afford. A great deal of money, for example, is spent on slimming aids and diet plans which might be spent to much greater effect on organically grown vegetables since fresh vegetables are an ideal food for those concerned about their weight. Only rarely do they contain appreciable amounts of fat and, in any case, vegetables, particularly when they are eaten raw in salads, contain dietary fibre which contributes to general health, digestion and weight control.

The salad recipes given in chapter six provide an excellent basis for a healthy diet, though the dressings, especially the mayonnaise dressings, would need to be used in moderation in a calorie controlled diet . There would be no need to give up potatoes since these in themselves contain negligible fats. The real problem with potatoes lies in the ways they are cooked and served. Frying in lard or oil increases the fat content dramatically; so does serving them with butter or melted cheese. Baked potatoes with a low fat yogurt dressing on the other hand are quite acceptable in a low calorie diet.

One problem with any weight control diet is that the act of chewing itself produces enzymes which activate digestion and can contribute to hunger. Also, some diets seem to take a depressingly long time to have a noticeable effect. A more drastic approach to the problem is a 'cleansing diet' or fast. Many cultures and religions that have a more spiritual approach to food than our own include periods of fasting during their annual calendar and a period without meals of solid food has benefits beyond that of weight reduction. For the fortunate population in the richer parts of the world the gut is continually dealing with food taken in by regular eating, often providing far more than the body actually needs. It follows that the whole metabolic process is then disproportionately involved with this luxury intake of nutrient, from the brain to the alimentary canal. The affects are noticeable in disturbed sleep, indigestion, constipation and, perhaps, a general feeling of either hyperactivity from an excess of sugars and caffeine, or lethargy when the body is digesting large amounts of meat and proteins. A period of fasting allows the body to clear out the alimentary canal and relieves the workload on many other organs. General energy and mental alertness result and the effects can often be seen in a person's face and complexion. Some people describe fasting as like being on a high with unusual rates of mental activity and as the processes of cooking and eating are absent there is a general gain in time throughout the day.

In all our discussions about food and eating nothing causes as much controversy as fasting. Many people seem really angry at the idea and delight in discovering that our own fasts include some food intake like soup and fruit juices and they seem to think they have caught us out. Other people can't imagine the discipline of going without food even for one day, and others say that periods without food are impossible, causing dizziness, headaches and tiredness. Quite understandably many older people who have lived through periods of food shortages like the Second World War feel affronted at the idea of choosing not to eat since, for their generation, regular meals are synonymous with good health. In reality, during rationing and wartime food shortages the general health of the population at large improved, a fact that nutritionists attribute to the actual restricted and often more wholesome vegetable based diets that people ate. After all, rats apparently live longer and far healthier, if kept half-starved.

Some words of caution are necessary, however. Any drastic change in eating habits can cause problems and a sudden crash diet or fast could be dangerous for some people. Anyone with a medical condition should be careful about dieting and fasting, and for those who do try a fast, heavy and manual work should be avoided for the duration as should stimulants like tea, coffee, alcohol and tobacco. Our own fasting follows the ideas of Barbara's uncle Port, a cultured and philosophical man who enjoyed food and wine, but who undertook a fast each season of the year.

A five day cleansing diet

Day 1. The first day is in preparation for the stricter fast to come and the diet consists of fruit and salads but with no carbohydrates or dairy products; say for breakfast, fruit and fruit juice; lunch – salad; and then for supper, salad, fruit salad and herb tea.

Day 2 to Day 4. These are the fast days when no solids are eaten at all. The day should start with fresh pressed fruit juice and at lunch and dinner time a clear, strained soup with no trace of solids. Freshly pressed fruit juices and herb and fruit teas sweetened with honey can be drunk throughout the day, and as you feel you need them. Day 2, the first day without solids, is by far the most difficult, but if the fast works for you, by Day 3 things are really improving, hunger pangs are less acute and the soup and fruit juices taste divine. By Day 4 the benefits should definitely be felt in mind and body and the anticipation of returning to regular meals is tempered by a sadness at losing the alertness, clarity and sense of achievement that comes during fasting.

Day 5 is preparing for a return to normal eating habits, and like Day 1 the menu comprises fruit and salads.

The first fast is the most difficult. Subsequent ones become easier and more beneficial and you become used to the patterns that develop over the five days. If they seem really beneficial and pose no problem, the diet can be extended to seven days, again with the first and the last day being the days of fruit and salad.

These cleansing diets can be a useful part of weight control and certainly by the end of even one five day fast the distended belly is under control again. Also following a five day fast hunger is more easily satiated. A more rigorous experience is offered by Christoph Michl who organises 'fasting walks', where groups hike through beautiful parts of Europe like the Black Forest, the Italian Alps, and Snowdonia covering up to 15 miles a day, drinking only water, tea and vegetable soup and eating no solids.

Part two

MORE THAN JUST SALADS

CHAPTER 4

Salad for all seasons

WRITING IN *Country Living,* Anne Boston made the point that the salads from our shop in Aberystwyth were *"decidedly not the penitential roughage variety"* and this underlines a simple idea: that nutritious food should be enjoyable, and that salads should have a zest and verve with the right combination of vegetables and herbs to give a blend of textures, flavours and colour. We use fresh herbs and edible flowers since they transform the quality of food, improve the flavour, contribute to health and aid digestion. This is also true of the sharp and bitter flavours of some of the leaf vegetables we use like the endives and chicories. As the national diet has become increasingly bland less and less food with a distinctive taste is eaten. Yet these traditional foods, and the bitter tastes in particular, stimulate enzymes which aid digestion and the more they are absent from our food the more we come to rely on pharmaceutical medicines to cure digestive disorders.

Mixed leaf salad

THERE ARE a tremendous number of leafy plants that can be used in salads besides the usual lettuces and endives. Some are very old plants known to gardeners for centuries, some have been sadly neglected but many are enjoying a revival of interest. There are also plants that grow wild, leafy plants from the herb garden, and newer introductions of oriental vegetables.

Lettuces

The traditional round butterhead lettuce is still the most widely available. In the winter and early spring short day varieties are produced in greenhouses and the larger outdoor varieties are usually ready in May and June and continue cropping until the autumn when they succumb to mildew and the cold and damp and are finally killed off by the frost. Perhaps the most enjoyable of these lettuces are the first home grown ones in the spring, and a February planting in greenhouses or polytunnels will usually allow lettuces to be cut from Easter onwards. As with most leaf salads the best of these lettuces are those grown quickly with plenty of warmth, light and fertility and harvested just as the hearts are fully formed. A well grown butterhead lettuce should be sweet, crisp and succulent and eaten as soon after harvest as possible.

Iceberg lettuces are now almost as common as butterhead ones. First developed in the Salinas valley in California iceberg lettuces are now widely grown in the summer in Britain and imported from Spain, France and Israel throughout the year. Iceberg is not in fact a variety of lettuce but a method of presentation, and many varieties of crisphead lettuce are grown for iceberg production. Few of the varieties have the flavour of the original crisphead Webbs Wonderful. This old variety is still a good choice for the gardener but is deemed too unreliable for commercial growers and doesn't make the large dense heads required for iceberg production.

Cos lettuce suffered greatly from the increased popularity of the iceberg, but there are now strong signs of its revival. Of all lettuces the small sugar cos, Little Gem, is often claimed to have the best flavour: sweet, nutty and crisp with no trace of bitterness so long as the plants are cut when still young. Little Gem is an excellent lettuce to grow in the spring and early summer, and with good growing conditions is usually ready six weeks from planting out. Later in the year as the days start to get shorter Little Gem is prone to mildew, so from midsummer onwards it is better for gardeners to switch to one of the larger cos varieties like Lobjoits Cos.

For added colour both in the garden and on the table there are several varieties of continental red lettuce. The red colour is due to the presence of anthocyanin in the leaf. The most versatile and easy to grow is Lollo Rosso, a crinkly red lettuce ideal for garnishing all manner of dishes but with an undistinguished flavour. The lettuce was named, of course, after La Lollo, the Italian actress Gina Lollobrigida, and there is also a green variety, Lollo Biondo. In recent years Lollo Rosso has become very popular with caterers and seems to be replacing iceberg as the first choice garnish in good restaurants and in airline food. Red Oak Leaf Salad Bowl, also available in a green variety, has a better flavour and is especially good in the autumn. It is a useful garden lettuce because it can be treated as a cut and come again lettuce, but for shop sales it poses a real problem, because like all open hearted lettuces, it wilts quickly after harvest. In the greengrocery trade it's known as a 'one day' lettuce, and nothing looks sadder than a wilted oak leaf lettuce after a day left on the shelf. Marvel of the Four Seasons is a red leaved butterhead variety which hearts up unlike the loose leaved salad bowl and lollo varieties. In our experience although it can grow into a very large lettuce it is once again better harvested early. The young lettuce have a deeper colour and a better flavour whilst the older hearted lettuces tend to suffer from basal rot which spoils the outer leaves and the heart. There are also red varieties of cos lettuce and plant breeders are constantly introducing new strains including red Batavian lettuces.

Endives and chicories

From autumn until the spring the endives and chicories provide colour and texture for winter salads. Endive Frisée is a hair trigger crop when grown in the summer for it suddenly becomes over-mature and rots from the base. Autumn and winter crops mature more slowly and they can be blanched by bunching up the leaves and tying them with raffia ten days before harvest. Rather less well known in Britain are the broad leaved endive or Batavian lettuces. These grow very large and stand well through the autumn, producing big creamy hearts with a flavour and texture similar to blanched chicory.

The best known chicory is Witloof, most of which is imported from Belgium and must be that country's largest vegetable export, although Belgian horticulture is also remarkable for its hothouse grown grapes and peaches. Witloof chicory is forced and blanched to produce the almost white chicons used most often in the classic chicory and orange salad. The Italian red chicory, Radiccio, with its marvellous deep red colours and dense crisp heads is also increasing in popularity. In Italy all chicories are known as Radiccio, but in Britain the term is reserved for the red leaved varieties. The seed company Suffolk Herbs introduced a full range of Radiccio seeds in 1980. The older varieties originate from the north east of Italy and carry the names of the towns around which they have been traditionally grown. Rossa Di Treviso has long, deep red pointed leaves. Although rarely available in shops, Treviso is a good winter standby for gardeners. The roots can be lifted and forced like Witloof chicory to give pale loose leaved chicons. This is a very old variety recorded in the 16th century. Rossa Di Verona produces a tight head in the winter and it can also be forced for chicons like Treviso. There are also red and green variegated forms which have loose heads, like Variegata di Castelfranco, Variegata di Choggi and Variegata di Sottomarina Precoce.

The main commercial variety of Radiccio is Palla Rossa and in recent years the Dutch commercial seedhouses have been 'cleaning up' the Italian varieties to produce a more standard cultivar with a dense head for commercial growers. The problem for large scale commercial production seems to be that the seeds from Italy perform very erratically giving open hearted, tight head, standard, red, green and variegated forms. For the amateur and the salad maker this is part of their charm and standardization can only reduce their appeal.

Leaf salads, salad herbs and cresses

The lettuces, endives and chicories provide the basis but many other salad plants and herbs can be added to enliven the mixed leaf salad. Early in the year from late February, sorrel leaves can be picked and their sharp lemony, slightly sour flavour adds a special character to the salad. It also makes an excellent soup. Sorrel is a hardy perennial, the wild form being found in most of the unimproved swards of Welsh grass farms. Garden sorrel, *rumex acetosa*, has narrow shaped leaves like the wild plant whereas the cultivated form French sorrel, *rumex scutatas* has broad leaves which widen at the base. Since by summer sorrel quickly runs to seed it is most useful in the spring.

In contrast to sorrel, corn salad, *valerianella locusta* or lamb's lettuce has a mild flavour but its dark green leaves are very nutritious; being a very hardy plant it is very valuable in midwinter and early spring. On the continent lamb's lettuce is known as Rapunzel from the fairy tale, since it was the search for this dark green winter salad that first led Rapunzel's father into the clutches of the witch. Lamb's lettuce and celeriac are a classic Franconian salad combination to have in the autumn with deep fried carp.

Claytonia, *claytonia perfoliata*, also called winter purslane (and sometimes miner's lettuce) is another mild flavoured winter salad. It is a small plant with thick succulent leaves and besides being an addition to the mixed leaf salad, small plants can be cut and served whole to make an interesting and unusual garnish. The dish that most exemplifies Barbara's culinary ideal is baked sewin served on a bed of claytonia, with boiled potatoes and a fresh green salad. The recipe, outlined later, uses local ingredients, and is simply prepared. The fish is cooked with herbs and served with salad. All in all it makes a delicious seasonal delicacy.

In the Puntazzo Restaurant on Stromboli no salad is complete without rocket, *eruca sativa*. Very popular throughout Italy, *rocula* is an important ingredient of *insalata mista*, or mixed salad. In the vegetable markets of Italian towns bunches of fresh rocket are sold alongside the other ingredients like Treviso and Palla Rosso radiccio. Although thought of today as a Mediterranean salad herb, rocket was well established in Britain by the beginning of the 14th century, and one of the first writers on salads, the diarist and philosopher John Evelyn (1620 – 1706),was growing it at his garden at Says Court, Deptford, in the 17th century. Rocket has a spicy, peppery taste and you either love it or you hate it. An Italian friend of ours, now living in London, is always pestering us to get some to her, whereas Barbara's brother, Stefan, can't abide it. One year we sent some seeds of rocket, mizuna and land cress to be grown in his restaurant's herb garden for use in their mixed herb and cress salads, but Stefan banned the use of rocket calling it, in typical forceful fashion, 'stinkcress'. Rocket is easy to grow, which is just as well since if you do like it you'll find that it's rarely available in shops. Sow it in the spring or late summer for a crop that will stand the winter in a cold greenhouse. Pick off the leaves as you need them and although the plant will eventually flower it can be cut back to encourage more leafy growth. Besides being a distinctive addition to the mixed leaf salad, Rocket also combines well with mushrooms and avocados. The white flowers of rocket are too hot to be edible, but the ornamental form, sweet rocket, has excellent mild tasting white flowers for use as a garnish.

Oriental salads

MIZUNA IS A JAPANESE mustard with fern-like leaves, one of the many ornamental vegetables that Joy Larkcom has popularised in her books *The Salad Garden* and *Oriental Vegetables*. It has a mild flavour not unlike chinese cabbage, but it is more subtle and can be grown readily throughout the year. The leaves make an attractive garnish and mizuna is very useful in late autumn when other salad crops are becoming less available.

Chinese cabbage is also at its best from late summer through to mid winter since this is when the garden and home grown crops are available. Since the popularity of chinese leaves has become so well established chinese cabbage is imported year round from Israel (where the Chinese Leaves name was first used), Portugal, Austria, Spain and France. Another oriental vegetable suitable for salad or for cooking is pak choi. This is a mild flavoured and succulent form of chinese cabbage, but quite different from the varieties grown for chinese leaves. Whereas Chinese leaves varieties have very crinkly textured leaves, pak choi has bright green, round, glossy leaves. Like Chinese leaves pak choi is very good stir fried, and in its raw form useful as part of a mixed leaf salad or on its own with cherry tomatoes.

In their catalogues seed companies have not always made the distinction between pak choi and Chinese leaf varieties completely clear , and one year we grew a thousand chinese cabbages all of which turned out to be pak choi. Unfortunately the demand for pak choi is much more limited than for Chinese leaves and we certainly couldn't use all the plants in the Salad Shop. We grew the pak choi in Cae Cartws, a gently sloping field overlooking Cwm Mabws and so called because when Ty'n yr Helyg was worked by horse power this field was closest to the building where the carts were kept. Although a very stony field Cae Cartws is inherently productive and the Pak Choi plants grew very strongly, most of them weighing several pounds even when trimmed for sale.

Sadly sales were sluggish at first and the crop reached maturity and then looked in danger of bolting and going to seed. Then, suddenly, sales in Aberystwyth started to increase, not dramatically but steadily. In fact the pak choi were being bought up by a family from the Mandarin Chinese Restaurant in Pier Street. They were so pleased with them that they asked if they could come to the fields and pick their own to store for the winter as their grandparents had done in China. And so it was that on a bright afternoon in early autumn three generations of the family arrived in two cars and proceeded to the field to harvest pak choi. It was a memorable cameo, an extended Chinese family picking chinese cabbage in Cwm Mabws, with behind them Cardigan Bay and the faint horizon of Bardsey Island and the Llŷn Peninsula.

Wild plants

ON THE CONTINENT many wild plants are used in salads and it's a common sight in spring in France to see young dandelion leaves being collected for the salad bowl. There's also a history of using wild plants in Britain. In her immensely entertaining study *Consuming Passions*, a history of English food and sexual appetite, Philippa Pullar catalogues the huge variety of plants that have been eaten over the centuries. In medieval times, for example, dandelions were eaten in the spring together with dock leaves, nettles and the budding leaves of hawthorn. As John Evelyn was later to remark, *"Every hedge affords a sallet"*. In our own times Joy Larkcom and Richard Mabey have both championed the use of wild plants in salads.

Many of our garden plants are cultivated forms of their wild relatives. Sorrel is a case in point, land cress another. Many forms of cress are useful in the mixed leaf salad. Mustard cress and watercress are most often available in shops, although commercial salad cress in the familiar punnets is usually sprouted rape seed. American or land cress is safest to grow in the garden since there is a danger of infection from the parasitic liver fluke from water cress grown near sheep pastures, and that means just about all of west Wales. The Watercress Growers Association guarantees that all watercress sold by its members is grown in pure spring water beds. Land Cress, which can easily be grown in a moist shady corner of the garden, or in a cool greenhouse throughout the winter, is the best alternative for gardeners. We've also used the wild shepherds cress, *teesdalia nudicaulis,* which self-seeds in the polytunnels and is ready for use early in February. The young plants are tender and full of flavour, good both for the mixed salad bowl or mixed with celeriac in an oil and vinegar dressing.

Whatever combination of leaf salads are used, parsley, lemon balm, mint, and chives can also be chopped into the salad to spice up the flavour, and the bowl finally garnished with edible flowers.

Herbs and edible flowers

CONTEMPORARY MEDICAL research confirms the importance of fresh fruit and vegetables in promoting health. As a general rule, eating two fruits and three vegetables each day is held to be beneficial in the prevention of degenerative disorders. A wide range of foods provides a variety of vitamins and nutrients, but the particular importance of plant foods is that they contain dietary fibre, and the different forms of fibre in various fruit and vegetables perform different beneficial functions. Herbs are a special case and their value as natural medicines has been known for centuries. Rich in vitamins, many herbs also contribute to health as natural germicides and antiseptics, besides aiding digestion and assisting in cleansing the body of toxins. Apart from their role in health, herbs also contribute to the taste, flavour and aroma of food, and this is as true for salads as for cooked food.

Many classic combinations are well known: cucumbers and dill, new potatoes and chives, tomato and basil. In Germany, winter savoury *(satureja nontana)* is known as the 'bean herb' and a sprig is always added when beans are cooked. Sweet cicely *(myrrhis odorata)*, which grows early in the year, is very useful to cook with rhubarb as it counteracts the tartness that comes from the oxalic acid in rhubarb, and reduces the amount of sugar needed to sweeten the cooked fruit. Moreover a soup simply made from fresh herbs with cream and white wine is also an excellent light and delicious starter for any meal. We use herbs extensively in our salad recipes and we recommend those we have found best to compliment the particular vegetable ingredient. For example we use lovage with cooked carrot salads, but chervil with grated raw carrots.

Throughout the year many herbs can be substituted depending on their seasonal availability and parsley is the great year round standby. In our gardens we grow the moss-curled varieties of parsley and also the broad-leaved kind which is known variously as 'French' 'Italian' or 'Continental' parsley. On the continent it is known as soup-parsley since although it is not so attractive for use as a garnish it has a stronger flavour and so is particularly useful in cooking.

Edible flowers

Flowers also contribute to the appeal of the salad; however, apart from their colour and attraction many of the edible flowers are well known to herbalists for their medicinal properties. For example marigold, *calendula officinalis,* is a very useful plant, flowering, as its botanical name suggests, throughout most of the year. Its yellow/orange petals are wonderfully ornamental on salads and it has been used as a healing herb since medieval times. Nasturtium, *tropaeolum minus,* grows rampantly during the summer months. It is rich in vitamin C and is beneficial for the stomach and intestines and guards against infections. The leaves, and especially the flowers, are used extensively as garnishes for summer salads. Borage, *borago officinalis,* is another strong-growing summer annual whose tiny deep blue flowers are a striking garnish. Herbalists claim the plant as a blood purifier maintaining its potassium content gives it diuretic properties, whilst the flowers act as a heart tonic. There are a large number of edible flowers to use in salads including bergamot, borage, camomile, chicory, chives, sage, hyssop, lavender, mallow, marjoram, marigold, nasturtium, pelargonium, rose, rosemary, sweet rocket and viola.

Salads through the seasons

Spring salads

Spring in west Wales is *gwanwyn,* lamb time. A magical time of lambs and daffodils, curlews and buzzards, when gardens, as in the West Country, seem to look their best before the rampant growth of summer. We expect salads in spring, when the palate yearns for fresh young leaves and the appeal of *cawl cennin,* casseroles and winter stews begins to pall. Ironically, despite the anticipation, spring is a time of shortage, when the last of the field vegetables are cleared ready to plough for the new season crops, and when the stored root vegetables are nearing the end and their quality deteriorating. Until quite recently late spring/early summer was a time of real shortages, when the 'hungry gap' was only bridged by a few fresh vegetables like early purple sprouting broccoli and 'hungry gap' kale. Gardeners employed techniques of forcing early crops on hot beds and under bell-jars and cloches, techniques that reached their zenith in the Victorian kitchen garden. Today all of that has largely been consigned to a position of novelty and historical interest, since imports from overseas and the use of heated greenhouse growing systems mean that the seasonal hungry gap is hardly noticeable to the majority of supermarket shoppers, except perhaps for the much higher prices at this time of year.

Nevertheless the first lettuces and herbs for use in the mixed leaf salad are eagerly awaited in the spring. Chives are one of the earliest herbs to show and they grow quickly from February onwards. Clumps of chives can be dug from the garden and brought into the greenhouse or to the kitchen window sill. Especially if they have had a frost in the garden, the chives will respond to the sudden change in temperature and grow very strongly. Besides being used in the mixed leaf salad and on new potatoes chives go very well in a mushroom salad.

The earliest root vegetables are radishes, spring onions and the first young carrots and beetroots. Radishes are the fastest growing vegetable and can be raised early in the garden, in a cool greenhouse or under cloches. New season radishes combine very well with sprouted alfalfa, their sharpness contrasting with alfalfa's flavour of mild young peas. The round red varieties like Scarlet Globe and Cherry Belle are best for chopping into alfalfa salad, whereas the longer French Breakfast, which is a white variety with a deep red, or red and purple flushed shoulder, is better for serving on its own with salt or in addition to other salads. In Franconia long white radishes are served in pubs with salt to eat with a glass of beer in contrast to our tradition of potato crisps. The best variety to grow for these is White Icicle.

Spring onions can be available very early in the year. Overwintered White Lisbon varieties are ready in early spring, and spring sown ones are ready for pulling by June, especially if given cloche protection. We find that the cool damp winters of west Wales are unsuitable for overwintering spring onions, and indeed many other crops. Our first salad onions come from the perennial Welsh onion, *allium fistulosum* and from tree onions, *allium cepa aggregatum*. Both of these can be grown from seed and they subsequently form offsets underground and soon grow into large clumps. Both varieties are very hardy. The Welsh onion comes originally from Siberia, the name 'Welsh' deriving from the Old English 'Waelisc' meaning 'foreign', whereas the tree onion is a native of Canada. Besides multiplying by offsets the tree onion also produces small cocktail-onions in bunches on the end of its stems. The real value of these onions is that they produce green shoots or 'chibols' for use as spring onions very early in the year.

When other salad vegetables are in short supply, beansprouts are a very useful and nutritious standby. Sprouted seeds are particularly high in vitamins and minerals, especially iron, potassium and iodine. Seeds can be sprouted in a jar with a muslin cover or a proprietary seed sprouter. We've successfully used a glass sweet jar with a milk filter secured over the top by a rubber band. To sprout successfully the temperature needs to be constantly 55°-70°F, and the sprouting seeds need to be thoroughly rinsed twice a day. Most are ready to eat within four to six days and for crisp white beansprouts the jars are best kept in the dark. All manner of seeds can be sprouted in this way, including chick peas, haricot beans, mung beans, alfalfa, radish and fenugreek.

Salad cress and mustard can be grown and cut as seedlings for salad, but for an interesting variation sunflower seeds can be used as a seedling 'sprouted' crop. The seeds are sown in a tray of compost, or in a small container. When the young plants are two or three inches high and just as they are about to form their first true leaves, cut them down and use in salads. They are marvellously crunchy.

As spring progresses the first carrots and beetroot are available from the garden or sold in shops in bunches. Tender and sweet, they are the first sign that the 'hungry gap' is nearly over.

Summer salads

Welsh spring weather is unpredictable to say the least. The vagaries of the weather make it seem that whereas some springs come early, others come late with a definite tendency in recent years for late springs. No matter how hard we try to advance spring crops by early sowings and plantings, by the use of cloches and 'floating film' mulches, and by taking advantage of warm sunny spells early in the year, the first real flush of vegetables rarely comes on stream for harvest until the second week of July. Our garden diary reveals sad stories of crops planted out during a warm week in March only to be blasted by icy winds in April with, *"...a sudden return to arctic weather, snow and north east winds"*.

In some previous years, when the weather has been dry and mild we have planted out potatoes in February. By May the potatoes have been well advanced but then sudden late frosts have turned the haulms black and ruined the crop. Now we delay potato planting until the last week of March or the first week of April. The spell of cold weather in May is a regular visitor, and in Franconia these 'Holy Ice Men' are always expected between the 10th and 14th of May. In Britain this feature of the weather is known as 'Buchan's Cold Spells' after the Scottish meteorologist who observed the pattern in the 19th century. So over the years we've learned to work and garden with the seasons and to wait until early summer for the first real vegetable harvest.

As July progresses into August more crops become ready: peas, beans, courgettes and spinach and, from the greenhouse, tomatoes, cucumbers, peppers and melons. Salad vegetables need to be fresh and in season to enjoy them at their best, when their flavour and texture are at their peak. Using poor quality produce is like making a flower arrangement with wilted blooms, and no one, as the chef Raymond Blanc has pointed out, would ever dream of doing that. The classic ingredients of the traditional summer salad, tomatoes and cucumbers are good examples. So many people complain that tomatoes no longer have any flavour, even though they are able to buy perfectly round red fruits for 13 months of the year. Varieties and techniques have been developed to produce tomatoes of consistent size and appearance throughout the year, but appearance and yield have been achieved at the expense of flavour. No wonder perhaps that customers are prepared to pay much higher prices for the flavour of tiny cherry tomatoes. Even this market is now in jeopardy as plant breeders and growers develop new commercial varieties which are easier to grow, have more standard shaped fruit and are easier to pick and pack than the traditional variety Gardener's Delight. Some of these newer varieties often lack the real cherry tomato flavour.

In Lampeter, Ceredigion, where Organic Farm Foods (Wales) have their packhouse, the company imported large marmande type tomatoes from France which were excellent in flavour and for slicing in salads. During a visit to the packhouse the supermarket buyers declined to buy them because the colours and shapes did not meet their specifications. Later, at lunch however, they were very complimentary about the wonderful flavour of the tomatoes, ironically enough the same ones they had just rejected as unsuitable for their stores.

Tomatoes, which are indigenous to the Andes in South America, are not an easy crop to grow commercially in the cool climate of west Wales. This area has low light levels compared to the main production areas of southern coastal England, and tomatoes grown indoors prefer the buoyant atmosphere of glasshouses to polythene tunnels. The cost of erecting commercial sized greenhouses, however, is a considerable investment and a dangerous one in an area exposed to frequent strong winds. Nonetheless many organic growers persist with the crop, especially in the coastal area between Llanrhystud and Aberaeron, and organically grown local tomatoes with all the delights of freshness and flavour are available in season, usually from July to October.

Cucumbers, a crop originally from India, are more easy to grow locally, and despite problems with mildew they can successfully be grown in polythene tunnels. The local organic product is quite different from the shrink-wrapped conventional cucumber. In Birmingham wholesale market there are large stands devoted almost entirely to cucumbers in the summer months and as one salesman reported, all of their growers now use rockwool as a growing medium, with not one using traditional soil beds. *"They look wonderful and straight"*, he volunteered, *"but they don't taste of anything."* At home at Ty'n yr Helyg our children go in summer to the polytunnels and pick off cucumbers to eat like melons, crisp and sweet. Making salads for our shop we also noticed the difference. The local organic fruit smells strongly of cucumber and when it's chopped the bowl is simply full of crisp slices. Take the conventional cucumber and do the same thing, and you find that the aroma of cucumber is virtually non-existent and at the end of slicing the bowl is half full of water. As with so many crops the extra size and yield achieved by artificial growing techniques and chemical fertilisers is nothing more than the uptake of extra water. The vegetables may appear cheaper to the customer but they're actually buying a higher water content than in the naturally grown product.

At home, the well-organised gardener has sown successive crops of lettuce, radish and spring onions and the fruit garden harvest moves from rhubarb, virtually the only home grown fruit in the first six months of the year, to strawberries, gooseberries, red and white currants, blackcurrants and raspberries. By August the first apples are ready for picking, old varieties like Beauty of Bath and George Cave, and the successful, new early apple, Discovery. Towards the end of summer come the plums, the small early variety Czar, and later the great favourite Victoria, followed by the late varieties like Majories Seedling.

Besides salad from the garden, during the summer fruit salad and drinks can be made with the season's produce. Fresh basil and dill are available from the herb garden and some of the tiny blue borage flowers can be frozen in ice cubes to add a splash of zest to cool summer drinks; meanwhile the choice of edible flowers for garnishing is endless

Autumn salads

If August is the month of summer's abundance, then September is the month of the autumn glut. Traditionally, the September surplus was pickled, salted and stored for the winter. Although the deep freeze has replaced the storage cellar and the vegetable clamp, many of the pickle recipes still have their place and vegetables preserved in the time of plenty can be enjoyed with salads throughout the autumn and winter. For example, cucumber 'bread and butter' pickle is a wonderful way to use up the small cucumbers left on the plants at the end of the season.

As the weather cools and the days get shorter with the first early frosts the summer vegetables start to fail. Autumn salads reflect the seasonally available crops, using leeks and celeriac and the hardy leaf salads, Chinese cabbage, the endives, chicories and lamb's lettuce. Though now available throughout the year, celery is a traditional autumn crop. It is a very demanding crop to grow well, requiring good supplies of nitrogen for the initial growth, and ample available potash for the celery to mature and grow thick, crisp sticks. Modern celery is of two kinds, the white self-blanching varieties available mostly in spring and summer, and the American green varieties common in autumn and winter. A great deal of celery is imported to keep up the year round supplies, with early season crops from Spain and the Channel Islands, and the green kind imported from Israel through the winter. In the past, celery was grown in trenches and blanched by earthing up around the plants to produce the crisp white sticks. Until quite recently the best 'dirty celery' appeared in the wholesale markets in the early autumn still carrying evidence of the black peaty soils in which it was grown, especially in the Cambridgeshire fens and the Ormskirk region of Lancashire.

Carrots are a useful basis for autumn salads and they go very well with celery and chopped peppers. Maincrop carrots are harvested from September onwards and Chantenay and Autumn King are good flavoured traditional varieties, although most commercial growers now use F¹ hybrid varieties. Carrots are the crop which it is claimed first made a commercial impact for organically grown produce. Certainly in west Wales it was the first crop to be grown on anything like a large scale, a scale that required marketing beyond farm gate sales and deliveries to local shops and restaurants. Peter Segger at Blaencarmel farm, Cilcennin, and Charles Wacher at Aeron Parc, Llangeitho, both grew carrots as part of their vegetable rotations from the mid 1970s, but it was Patrick Holden at Bwlchwernen Fawr, Llwyn-y-groes, who really led the way in field scale carrot production as a diversification from dairying, and pioneered the sales to distant London markets and eventually the supermarkets. His brother Roger Holden continued the trend as did Mathew Murton at Crynfryn Farm in Pen-uwch. Maincrop organically-grown carrots are now available from many parts of west and south Wales and from Herefordshire, with imports from Spain, Portugal and Israel throughout the year.

Red apples give colour, texture and fruit flavours to many autumn salads. Unfortunately there is widespread prejudice against red skinned apples generally and many people think they all have poor flavour and a mealy, floury, soft texture. Whilst this may be true of some French and Italian varieties, especially after long periods in store, there are some very good red apples. One of the best early autumn apples is Spartan. This is a dark mahogany, almost dull purple apple, with a rich bloom. The flesh is white and crisp, very juicy with a sweet pleasant flavour. First raised in 1926 in British Columbia, Canada, this is now a good quality UK commercial apple and for many years Spartan won the Marden 'most eatable apple' competition. This is one of the many varieties of apple grown by

Ian and Rebecca Pardoe in Putley, Herefordshire, who have converted their orchards to organic cultivation. They also grow another late red apple, Idared, which keeps well into the New Year. Originally raised in Idaho, USA, Idared is primarily grown as a pollinator for Cox's Orange Pippin but it is a good dessert apple in its own right. Cox itself is very difficult to grow organically, which is a tragedy.

In spring and early summer, when home-grown apples are out of season, another American red apple, Red Delicious is available. Originating from about 1880 there are now some wonderful deep red clones of this apple grown organically in Washington State on the north Pacific coast of the USA. These organically-grown Red Delicious are firm and juicy, aromatic with a nutty flavour.

Winter salads

Winter in west Wales can be a fairly rigorous experience, but the coastal area rarely suffers extreme cold and prolonged periods of snow. There have been two exceptional years since the war: 1947 and 1981-2. In 1981-2 there were two blizzards one month apart, and both at full moon. Like many households, we at Ty'n yr Helyg were snowed in and the roads were impassably blocked by snow for ten days. Fortunately we had fuel for the fires, the hens continued to lay eggs, the goats were in milk, and we had in store flour for bread and sacks of potatoes, carrots, onions and some cabbage. Outside the glass greenhouse was comprehensively demolished by the second blizzard, but the polythene tunnels withstood everything the weather threw at them. Older people say that the winter of 1947 was rather worse with more snow and road communications blocked for much longer than in 1982. The snow lay in drifts much longer in 1947 and it is even said that when the hill farmers of Mynydd Bach were making hay in June the last remains of the snow drifts were still lying under north facing hedges.

Ironically, in 1947 country people were better placed to face being snowed in than in 1981-2. In those days farms produced a wider range of food and country people stored and clamped crops as a matter of course to see them through the winter. By the 1980s most farms were producing milk, beef, sheep and animal feed but little in the way of vegetables, and farmers like other householders were relying on shopping trips for their own foodstuffs. In 1982 outlying areas like Trefenter in Mynydd Bach had food airlifted in by helicopter.

Soups, stews and roast dinners are very much the images of winter food, but apart from exceptional times like 1947 and 1981-2 there are always possibilities for winter salads using fresh produce. By 1689 John Evelyn was able to pick a fresh green salad every day of the year from the garden in Sayes Court that he had established in 1653, and as the Rapunzel fairy tale shows, green salads have been prized in the winter for centuries.

Increasingly, winter salads are popular and the interesting leafy salad is now sought out by many people even as an addition to the traditional Dickensian Christmas dinner. Winter salads are imported from Israel, Spain, Egypt and Italy, but a carefully organised garden, especially one with a greenhouse or polytunnel, can still provide cabbages, broccoli, endives, chicory and herbs for fresh salad throughout the winter.

CHAPTER 5

Making a meal of it

IT TAKES little to turn a simple salad into a complete meal; just potatoes or bread, the right dressing, a dessert from seasonal fruit and a glass of whatever takes your fancy.

Potatoes

"The simpleton farmer grows the biggest potatoes" (Franconian proverb)

VIRTUALLY ALL vegetables can be eaten raw in salads, though only the most dedicated devotee of raw food uses swedes, parsnips and brussels sprouts. Potatoes however are the real exceptions being universally cooked before being eaten. In Britain, where the average adult eats something like two hundredweight of potatoes per year the vegetable constitutes an important source of essential amino-acids, vitamins and essential minerals to the national diet. Unfortunately vitamins C and Bl (Thiamine) are soluble in water, so unless the potatoes are cooked in their skins most of the vitamins will be poured away with the water. The usual ways of cooking are boiling, mashing, frying and baking, but there are many variations in the way they are prepared. One of the few clear memories I have of Ragusa in Sicily is sitting in a campsite near the beach one evening and watching the nearby Italian family prepare a meal. The Signora simply boiled potatoes in their skins, drained them, sliced them, and mixed them with coarsely chopped cloves of garlic. A liberal dousing of olive oil and they were ready to eat, and that, plus a green salad and a bottle of wine, was their supper. I couldn't wait to try it. Similarly, in the Canary Islands small potatoes are boiled whole in their skins in well salted water (traditionally sea water in fact) and served with a powdering of salt crystals. The skins go wrinkly which gives them their name, *papas arrugadas*.

When we visit Franconia it is noticeable that although potatoes are still a staple the most common ways of preparing them are *roest kartoffel*, where the parboiled potatoes are sliced, then lightly fried with onions and caraway or sesame seed, *knoedel*, a kind of potato dumpling, and potato salad.

Potato salad

The two requirements for potatoes to use in salad are flavour and texture. Potatoes vary widely in terms of cooking quality depending on the variety and where and how the crop was grown. Potatoes seem to be one of those vegetables where there is an inverse relationship between flavour and fertility: the more fertilised the soil in which the potatoes are grown the more watery and less flavour in the crop. Fortunately potatoes grown in the rather poor soils of west Wales have an outstanding flavour. Over the years we must have peeled tons of cooked potatoes when preparing them for salad, and it seems to be that generally speaking potatoes grown organically by market gardeners – who don't have as much farmyard manure or slurry available for their fields as farmers – produce the potatoes with the best flavour. The most watery, poor-flavoured potatoes on the other hand are those grown on heavily fertilised soils, often in areas known for producing high yields.

Flavour is rather subjective, but there is more agreement on texture and cooking quality. For potato salad the potato needs to be firm and waxy so that it can be sliced without disintegrating into a starchy pulp. Some varieties are particularly suitable for this, others highly unsuitable. In the case of floury potatoes the cells tend to separate from each other during cooking which makes them better for mashing and baking, whereas the moist waxy potatoes with more coherent tissues are better for potato salad. It is not known why the texture of varieties differ, in this way, though floury potatoes generally contain more starch.

We choose varieties that are firm, waxy textured and of good flavour, and for potato salad we cook them whole in their skins, then peel and slice them as soon as they're cool enough to handle. Usually we dress them with vinaigrette, but a mayonnaise dressing is richer. By preparing potato salad in this way most of the nutrients are retained, and as well as being a good addition to any salad meal it's an excellent accompaniment for fish, especially sewin and salmon, and freshwater fish like trout and carp. Because we don't include pasta, rice or pulses in our salads, potato salad is the main staple and source of carbohydrate, apart from bread.

Potato varieties

Potatoes were first brought to Europe by Spanish explorers around 1570 and they were introduced to England and Ireland, along with tobacco, by Sir John Hawkins and Sir Walter Raleigh. Raleigh cultivated potatoes on his estates in Ireland after bringing them back from his New England colony in Virginia at the end of the 1580s. By the second half of the 17th century they made their appearance in Wales, but it took a hundred years before they became the staple food of the majority of people in Cardiganshire.

In west Wales Pembrokeshire is famous for its early potatoes, and the history of Pembroke potatoes is closely linked to the Cardiff firm of Edward England Ltd. After the First World War Major Jack H England, the son of the founder of the firm, used to holiday in Pembrokeshire and he realised that the climate there was almost as mild as in Cornwall and Brittany. He was able to persuade a group of local farmers to experiment in growing early potatoes. The *Western Mail* of the time described the results as amazing and by 1935, 190 farmers had registered with Jack England's lucrative scheme, whereby he supplied the seed and guaranteed to market all their crop.

The main potato varieties grown in Pembrokeshire have been Home Guard (introduced in 1942), Ulster Sceptre (introduced in 1964) and Maris Bard (introduced in 1972). Unfortunately, despite its many advantages of earliness and flavour Home Guard in particular has poor cooking qualities. This is especially so when the crop is heavily fertilized, when it shows a tendency to go grey and to disintegrate, and this has given Pembrokes a poor reputation in some quarters. Maris Bard and Ulster Sceptre are better quality potatoes and each year new varieties are grown in the search for the ideal new potato. For some people the ideal already exists in the famous Jersey Royal (first introduced in 1879 as International Kidney), a kidney shaped potato with firm creamy yellow flesh, white skin and outstanding taste and flavour.

In Jersey potatoes are often planted as early in the year as January on the small, steep, south-facing enclosures known as cotils. Traditionally the Jerseymen fertilized their crops with seaweed just as farmers did in coastal areas of Ireland, Wales and Scotland. (Although it is free for the collecting and rich in nutrients, the possibility of contamination by nuclear waste discharged from Sellafield into the Irish Sea has put an end to its use locally). In Jersey farmers saved seed potatoes from each year's harvest, but they've been able to avoid degeneration of stocks because the seed was not grown on the same holding, but passed on to other farms in different parts of the island. This may well have helped to reduce the build up of disease in the stocks and to contribute to the distinctive character of the Jersey potato. Jersey first exported potatoes to the London markets in the 1880s and the success of the variety resulted in the Jersey States of Agriculture ordering that no variety could be exported for potato consumption other than the Jersey Royal.

Recently retailers have been selling potatoes by named variety, and some supermarkets have introduced some old favourites like Duke of York, Kerr's Pink and Pink Fir Apple. This is a marked improvement on the days when customers were simply offered 'reds' or 'whites'. Nonetheless, the choice is still rather limited in most stores to the main commercial varieties. In fact hundreds of potato varieties have been grown in Britain, and at the International Potato Centre in Peru over 4,000 varieties are maintained and grown. Although growers in this country constantly trial new varieties, many of the older varieties are being lost, largely due to the legislation which regulates the sales of vegetable seeds. Under the Seeds (National List of Varieties) Act of 1973 seed may only be sold if it is of a variety on the UK national list or in the EC's common catalogue. As Lawrence D Hills has shown in his *Good Potato Guide* the effect of this legislation has been to make many older varieties of vegetables, including potatoes, 'illegal'.

When we first started growing vegetables at Ty'n yr Helyg in the mid 1970s we drew heavily on the ideas of the organic gardener Lawrence Hills. The first potatoes we grew were Duke of York (introduced in 1891) and Record (1944), both recommended in his book *Grow your own fruit and vegetables*. These are good flavoured varieties but their texture is not ideal for salad. The seed came from Donald MacLean in Scotland who had the largest private collection of seed potatoes in the world, and who supplied small quantities by mail order. Sadly Donald MacLean died in 1988, the year we were trying to contact him again for varieties of seed potato suitable for salad.

Over the years we've tried a large number of varieties and we obtained small quantities of many different kinds from the University of Wales Potato Research Group who were also trialling them at their farms, Trefloyne, near Tenby, and Frongoch at Aberystwyth. In 1984, for example, we grew ten different varieties, and each year we tried whatever new ones the group had on offer and also sought other varieties from seedsmen. Although we now have some firm favourites that have good texture, flavour and crop well on our land, the quest continues. Among the varieties we have found particularly good for potato salad are Jersey Royal (1879), Estima (1973), Pink Fir Apple (1880), Vanessa (1968) and Desiree (1962). The French varieties Ratte (1972) and the recently introduced Charlotte are also excellent if you can obtain them. Many of these varieties also bake very well, and baked potato makes an excellent alternative accompaniment to salad. Other varieties that bake and roast well are King Edward VII (1902), Bintje (1910), Record (1925), and Marfona (1977).

Bread and baking

APART FROM winter rye, which we've grown to be grazed in the spring by sheep and goats, and then ploughed in as a green manure, we haven't grown cereals at Ty'n yr Helyg. This is mainly because, with only a small acreage that can be ploughed, we've concentrated on using this land to raise vegetables; however when I first contacted the local Soil Association group on arriving in west Wales, it was to discover that their main project at the time was to acquire and restore a mill and to produce organic flour. Since we were starting with just a small vegetable garden I could see no way of contributing to the venture, although when it transpired that the mill in question was one of the water mills in Llanrhystud I did toy with the idea of taking on the job of miller. In fact the water mill venture collapsed before it got started, but several stalwarts of the local Soil Association went on to grow wheat, notably at Bwlchwernen Fawr, Llwyn y groes; Aeron Parc, Llangeitho; Blaencarmel, Cilcennin; and Bryn-llys, Borth. The wheat was stone ground on an electric mill that was initially kept at Aeron Parc and it was sold locally under the Ceredigion Organic Growers label, but in the end the reality of the cool wet climate which cannot produce good quality milling wheat led to the whole venture being abandoned. Organic flour is still produced in mills in Wales but the wheat is imported from areas more suited to its cultivation, and some of the hard wheat for flour milling is imported from North America. In England some organic wheat producers established on-farm milling operations, notably Pimhill at Lea Hall Farm in Shropshire, Rushall Farm in Wiltshire and Doves Farm in Sussex. Doves Farm Flour, set up in 1978 by

Michael and Clare Marriage, is now the largest miller of organic cereals in the UK, and at its new site it has the second largest stone grinding mill in Britain, buying in organic wheat direct from other organic farmers.

Although potato salad was the main carbohydrate for the salads we prepared in the Salad Shop, our other essential has always been home-baked bread. For more than five years Barbara baked rolls and loaves for the shop and really only stopped when it became apparent that our home bakery could no longer comply with the increasingly stringent regulations governing food produced for sale.

Barbara's bread recipes use Dove's unbleached strong white flour (the use of chlorine dioxide to oxidise flour and to produce a uniform whiteness destroys some of its vitamin E) and Maesdulais brown flour. Although these flours can be used to bake either a brown or a white loaf, she's found that the best results come from a combination of the two, and at least one food journalist agreed, referring in a national magazine article to Barbara's delectably light home-baked rolls, made with organic wholemeal and unbleached white flour.

Many people have expressed surprise that our breads use white flour, but in fact the white flour versus brown flour argument is far from straightforward. White flour is produced by the grinding of wheat and the separation of the endosperm, germ and bran. The coarse fibrous particles, the germ and the bran, are sieved out leaving the refined or 'pure' white flour. The bran is particularly high in dietary fibre, 40-50 per cent, more than in other foods, so white flour is fibre-depleted flour. Wholemeal, or whole grain flour, is produced in the same way but the bran and the germ are added back in at the end of the process. In the case of wheats that are grown 'conventionally', ie using artificial fertilisers and chemical sprays, there is an argument that says that it is the outer coating of the grains that are most likely to absorb toxins from hormone weed-killers and fungicides. So wholemeal flour is more likely to contain chemical residues than white flour. In the case of organically grown wheat however, the use of all spray chemicals and artificial fertilizers are banned, so this argument is irrelevant.

What is well established is that the removal of the bran from flour results in the loss of fibre, and the removal of the germ means a loss of B vitamins. Furthermore there is also an overall loss of oil and as much as a 25 per cent loss of protein in white flour. The history of flour making shows a great conflict of interests between nutritionists and millers which in recent historical times has been reflected in legislation governing the vitamin content of bread, and at times, subsidized support for brown bread. With the overall decline in dietary fibre in our food, nutritionists have emphasised the value of wholemeal bread, and in recent years it has taken an increasing share of the market.

It is still the case, however, that bran and germ do reduce the bread-making qualities of flour, and many of our favourite baked foods like pizza, stollen and apfel strudel are just not the same when they're made with wholemeal flour: it is too heavy, too coarse; and because of its higher oil content its also true that brown flour doesn't keep as long as white flour. It has also been suggested that many more of the nutrients in whole grain flour actually pass through the body without being absorbed than those in white flour and in his detailed discussion of the subject in *On food and cooking*, Harold McGee concludes that, *"brown bread contains more nutrients than white bread but makes it more difficult to absorb them"*. So, in conclusion, the mixture of different wheat flours for bread baking seems a reasonable approach, so long as they are all unbleached and organically grown. The mixture of brown and white flours achieves a balance of available nutrients plus the presence of laxative dietary fibre.

Freshly baked bread is one of the oldest food delights in the European diet and home baking remains basically the same process it has been over the centuries. On Stromboli the pizzas at the Puntazzo restaurant were baked in a traditional stone oven, the kind that can be found throughout much of Italy. Sadly, the main theme in most of Europe is the closure of many of the small independent local bakeries that use traditional methods. Increasingly bread is produced by large industrialised bakeries, and sold through supermarkets. Some of what passes for bread is now a very inferior product, mechanically aerated with yeast simply added for flavour, kneaded in a food processor, and steam baked. This is in stark contrast to the manual tradition of home baking which involves preparing the yeast by adding it to warm water and a little sugar, kneading the dough to bring out the gluten content in the flour and to give it elasticity, rising the dough till it doubles in size with an even distribution of air and yeast, knocking back, which is a second round of kneading and removes excessive air bubbles in the bread, proving, which is when the loaves are left to rise again prior to baking, making quite sure that all the ingredients are evenly distributed to give the bread a good texture, and finally baking in a very hot oven, hot enough to kill off the yeast to stop any excessive rising.

Many of the large retail chains have discovered the value of in-house bakeries, with the enticing aroma of freshly baked bread wafting around the stores. An industry has developed to supply 'half-baked' loaves to these stores, but whatever the appeal of in-house supermarket bakeries they cannot replace the world of baking that we have lost.

During trips to France the bakeries and pâtisseries are generally the first ports of call, for croissants and baguettes. Delicious when fresh, they are made exclusively from white flour, and seem completely lacking in fibre. During my last visit I came to the conclusion that strong coffee, so essential to *le petit déjeuner*, is the vital laxative that serves as an antidote to the constipating effects of French bread. Ah, but we loved it. Some mornings when staying at Moulin de la Seguin in the Dordogne the house would be crowded with visitors who wanted to sleep late after an evening's revelry with food, music and wine, but my baby son would wake shortly after dawn and bellow for attention. So, with a thick head and heavy with sleep I rose with great difficulty, bundled him outside and into the car then drove to nearby Monpazier to stock up with croissants and fresh bread, returning to a hero's welcome from the slowly wakening household: croissants for breakfast, then sandwiches of cheese and lettuce, cucumber and mayonnaise for lunch.

In Germany, as in France and Italy, the main ingredient of *frühstück*, breakfast, is a wheat flour roll, or *brötchen*, and in Gasthaus Rottner Stefan has recently built a new pâtisserie to the highest of modern hygiene standards so that his guests can have the best fresh bread and pastries baked on the premises. Generally, however, ryebread rather than wheatbread has been the tradition in Franconia. Throughout middle Europe ryebread is the staple since rye grows well, standing the cold winters and dry summers better than wheat, and unlike oats, rye contains sufficient gluten for bread making. Sourdough bread is most common, and this is made without yeast. The first step in its preparation is therefore to make a 'starter' to raise the dough. This is made by fermenting some ryeflour in lukewarm water with buttermilk and caraway seeds. It takes four days to ferment, but once the starter has been made and used then some of the dough can be retained to use as a starter next time. Although the recipe for sourdough bread looks daunting it is actually quite straightforward if you have the time, and the bread keeps well and actually improves after a day or two. It also freezes successfully. Barbara's mother makes a loaf with linseed and walnuts added into the rye sourdough which results in a nutty, seedy bread full of flavour, texture and fibre.

Dressings and sauces

SALAD DRESSINGS enhance the appeal of lettuces and chopped vegetables by coating the surface area of the salad and giving it a special character and flavour. As a general rule all fresh leaf salads should be tossed in the dressing just prior to serving so that the salad stays crisp and succulent. Cooked vegetable salads on the other hand benefit from a period of marinating so that they can fully absorb the flavour. Our recipes are a series of variations on the two classic themes of vinaigrette and mayonnaise plus a yogurt dressing.

In European cooking the pre-eminence afforded to French cuisine is largely based on its 'grandes sauces' and these comprise two basic processes. One is the roux process where starch is thickened in butter to produce bechamel, veloute and espagnole sauces, and the other is the emulsion process which produces hollandaise, béarnaise, mayonnaise and vinaigrette. The last two stand rather apart since they are served with salads and cold food generally and use oil rather than butter. Mayonnaise is made with eggs and the other main ingredients in the recipes for salad dressings are vinegar, mustard, lemon juice, yogurt, and stock – the *fond de cuisine*.

Vinegar

The word vinegar is from the Old French *vinaigre* (modern French *vinegre*) which means sour wine, and vinegar is produced when alcoholic liquids like wine, cider, and fermented malt are soured by the acetobacter bacterium which turns the alcohol into acetic acid. As we and many other home cider and wine makers know to their cost this easily happens, especially when the vinegar fly gets into the fermenting jar. Wine vinegars are generally the best for salad dressings (though cider vinegars can also be used) and many writers seem to prefer red wine vinegar for vinaigrette to provide a colour contrast with the oil. In our salads we use herb and fruit flavoured white wine vinegars many of which have exceptional colours, quite surpassing those of red wine vinegar. The favourites are elderflower, raspberry and basil and we have also made strawberry, borage, tarragon, rosemary, sage and purple basil vinegars.

These flavoured vinegars are not difficult to prepare. For example we pick elderflower blossom on a sunny day when it is fully out in early summer. The florets are separated from the twigs and branches and then packed loosely into a jar and covered with white wine vinegar. An airtight lid is then screwed on and the elderflower is left to steep for three months in a cool dark place. By this time the vinegar will have completely absorbed the flavour of the elderflower and it can be strained into a bottle and labelled ready for use. The procedure for making other fruit and herb vinegars is much the same. The fruit or herbs should always be harvested on a dry day and any blemishes cut away before being packed into the jars and covered with the vinegar. Once bottled the flavoured vinegars will easily keep for a year and until the next season's batch are ready. When fresh herbs like basil are unavailable in mid-winter basil vinegar can still provide its essential flavour to dress a tomato salad.

Oil

Vegetable oils contain many important nutrients, particularly vitamins, but they also contain fatty acids and so some people have been tempted to reduce the oil content in their dressings. From a culinary point of view this is unfortunate because it is the oil that really coats the surface area of the salad and thereby imparts the flavour (for this reason it is also important to dry the salads well before dressing them because water and oil won't mix and wet lettuce leaves will repel the oil). From a health point of view it is also regrettable, since although oils may contain calories they tend to be low in saturated fats and high in unsaturated fats.

The classic oil for salad dressings is olive oil, produced throughout Mediterranean Europe, with many local variations, from Greece to Portugal. Some oils, particularly in Italy, are estate bottled whereas in France and Spain they may be marketed and labelled according to the region of production. In Portugal olives are fermented for some hours before pressing to produce a stronger flavoured oil, and friends of ours who live in the Algarve describe how villagers bring their family harvest to a communal press just as in France each commune will have its own wine press, and in Southern Germany villages have a communal apple press to make apfelsaft.

The finest olive oil is the extra virgin cold pressed oil. This is produced when the newly harvested whole olives are ground up and the oil extracted from the press by centrifugal force. This oil has the lowest level of acidity and although it keeps well it is at its best during the first year. Second and subsequent extractions are usually factory produced and have higher levels of acidity, and unfortunately many commercial processes now include high temperature pressing, bleaching, deodorising and the use of petroleum based solvents. With temperatures as high as 250°C, toxic effluents are produced and there is a loss of nutrients and flavour. Happily there are now a number of certified organic oils available and these are produced from organically grown olives (or grapeseed or sunflower seeds etc) and in the production process neither high temperature pressing nor solvent extraction is permitted.

Cold pressed olive oil has a particularly strong flavour which is fine with very strong flavoured salads made with, say, rocket or spring onions, but with mild flavoured salads the oil is overwhelming. The answer is to dilute the oil with a blander flavoured one like Safflower, or to use the really neutral flavoured grapeseed oil. Corn oil, walnut oil and sunflower oil can also be used in salad dressings.

Oils can be flavoured by a prolonged steeping of herbs like sage, thyme, rosemary and tarragon. Peppercorns, garlic, dill seed heads and juniper berries can also be included to make a mixed herb oil, but these are primarily for decoration. Most cold pressed oils are too strongly flavoured so a good refined oil like sunflower is best, but even so only the strongest herbs will actually flavour the oil. For milder herbs like dill and tarragon essences need to be used since the flavour of the oil will overpower the fresh herbs. A particularly interesting oil is made with dried mushrooms. Dried ceps or chanterelle are covered with oil and allowed to stand for at least three months by which time the oil has taken on the strong aroma of the fungi and is ready for use.

Mustard

Most recipes for salad dressings, if they are specific about the mustard to be used, specify Dijon mustard. Moutarde de Dijon has been famous since the 14th century and it has had an *appellation controlée*, like wines, since 1937; there are strict regulations controlling the ingredients and method of making what is generally regarded as the finest mustard in the world. There are other fine mustards, however. For example, elsewhere in France there is the whole grain Moutarde de Meaux which has been made in a traditional manner by monks since the 17th century. In Britain mustard has become synonymous with the name Colemans, and other mustards, like the celebrated 16th century thick, hot Tewkesbury mustard, have been lost without trace. Colemans' traditional mustard is bright yellow in colour with a hot and pungent taste. The colour is achieved by the addition of turmeric, and the flavour comes from a secret blending of white and brown mustard seeds.

Despite the fame and claims of Dijon, Meaux and Colemans we use two different mustards, one from Germany and one from Wales. The German mustard is a mild flavoured delicatessen mustard which is made with brandy wine vinegar, salt and spices, very suitable for vinaigrette dressings where the stronger Dijon or pungent Colemans would be too overpowering. The Welsh-made mustard is a whole grain mustard flavoured with wine vinegar, honey, salt and spices, and we use this to make a sweet and savoury mayonnaise dressing. Mustards can be easily made at home with the use of a food processor to grind the seeds. For English hot mustard use cold water, but for a milder and sweeter mustard mix the ground seeds with vinegar or grape juice.

Yogurt

Yogurt was first made in the Balkans from goat's milk, and is obtained by the rapid conversion of lactose (milk sugar) into lactic acid by the addition of the almost pure culture of the bacteria *lactobaccillus bulgaricus*. Milder and less acidic flavoured yogurts are now also made using *bifidus and acidophilus* cultures, although some commercially made products are merely acidified milk without any live bacteria used at all and these tend to have an inferior flavour, more preservatives and fewer vitamins and nutrients than live yogurts.

The west Wales area has seen a number of organic yogurt producers using both goat's milk and cow's milk, and during the many years we kept goats we made yogurt at home using some purchased live yogurt as a starter. In Aberystwyth Rachel's Dairy produces a range of wholemilk, low fat and Greekstyle yogurts from organic milk, particularly from their own herd of pedigree Guernsey cows at Bryn–llys Farm in Borth. We use yogurt to thin thick mayonnaise and to make a dressing in its own right.

Vinaigrette

The basis of vinaigrette is a blend of oil and vinegar in the proportions 3 to 1, with mustard, lemon juice, salt, pepper and sugar added according to taste. The addition of mustard and/or crushed garlic and chopped onion act as emulsifiers and stabilisers and help to thicken the dressing, though a thin dressing will coat the salad more readily. In our recipes we use a vegetable stock, herb vinegar and German mustard to give the dressing a particular flavour. We use sunflower oil in preference to olive oil since the strong flavour of olive oil tends to overpower the subtlety of the herb vinegar, and similarly we feel that Dijon mustard is too strong for vinaigrette. Moreover, some salads, especially the crisp textured and bitter flavoured ones made with endives and chicory, are best served with just a simple dressing of lemon juice and oil.

Mayonnaise

This is the classic Mediterranean dressing and although most authorities agree that the name comes from the Minorcan Port of Mahon, which was seized from the British by the Duc de Richelieu in 1756, Elisabeth Luard in her book on European peasant cookery suggests that it may also derive from the French word *'manier'*, to work by hand, or from the ancient Languedoc verb *'mahonner'*, to tire, just as modern French cookery uses the verb *'fatiguer'*, to tire a salad.

Mayonnaise is an emulsified sauce, but unlike hollandaise and bearnaise which are made with butter and served hot, it is made with eggs and oil and served cold. The basis is a blending of egg yolks, lemon juice, oil and seasoning. In the classic recipe the egg yolks are whisked first, and then the oil is added drop by drop as the sauce is continuously stirred to create an emulsion. In our recipes we use whole eggs which simplifies the procedure and eliminates the problem of what to do with the whites. We use a blender and the albumen from the egg white acts as a stabiliser and helps to prevent coagulation, which is the major problem to be avoided as the oil is whisked into the egg mixture until it emulsifies.

During the food scares over salmonella there were official health recommendations that no eggs should be eaten raw; however we have continued to make mayonnaise with fresh free-range eggs. Only the freshest eggs should be used since the lecithin content falls as the egg gets older, and it is the lecithin that promotes emulsion. Duck's eggs should definitely not be used raw since they are often laid in very wet, mucky conditions, and their more porous shells more easily permit infection. Our main concern about eggs centres on the confinement and feeding of battery flocks. Apart from the unspeakable conditions in which they're kept, battery hens are often fed on high protein rations which include processed 'recovered' chicken meat. If Salmonella is endemic in chicken flocks then this form of cannibalism will surely perpetuate it. Furthermore these feed rations may contain tartrazene, a colouring added by compounders to improve the yolk colour of hens denied access to fresh green-stuffs; and there is evidence that tartrazene, which is also used in some orange drinks, can cause allergic reactions in children and other vulnerable groups. We prefer to eat eggs from hens kept in clean free-range conditions and fed on pure grains and organic rations, but those who don't wish to use eggs at all can make a substitute mayonnaise by using tofu, and Pauline Burrows, that doyenne of cooks in the west Wales organic movement, uses tofu and tahini in her alternative mayonnaise recipes. Whatever recipe is followed it is preferable to use a glass, pottery, or stainless steel bowl and to avoid aluminium and iron because the metal oxides at the surface of these can cause discolouration of the pale sauce. Many cooks avoid aluminium in any case because this heavy metal has been suggested as a contributing factor in the development of Alztheimer's disease.

Fruit salad, desserts and drinks

Fruit salad

Fresh fruit salad was one of the most popular salads with customers in our shop, and one of the fastest sellers on warm, sunny days. Fortunately it's quite easy to prepare provided there are ready supplies of fruit. We used imported melon, banana, and oranges throughout the year and then added to the salad whatever fresh fruit was in season. From late spring to summer we had strawberries, then red and blackcurrants and finally raspberries from the fruit garden. In summer, of course, peaches and nectarines are plentiful. From autumn to winter we used blackberries, plums, apples and grapes. Although there's a dearth of local fruit in winter it's always possible to freeze some of the summer soft fruit surplus to supplement apples and imported fruit. When making the salad the fruit should be washed, peeled and chopped as required and then strained through a colander. Sugar is added according to taste, and sunflower seeds mixed into the salad give it an extra chewy dimension. Puréed bananas as a base, and a topping of cream or Greek style yogurt finish off the salad. Fresh fruit is an important source of nutrients, and although its high water content means that its dietary fibre is in a dilute form, it contains pectin which is not found in other foodstuffs, and it is suggested that a diet high in pectin can help the body excrete calories in the form of fat.

To avoid any likelihood of pesticide or fungicide residues choose organically grown fruit wherever possible. Fruit growers will maintain that all the spray chemicals are harmless and that, anyway, there is a harvest interval between spraying and picking. Unfortunately we hear too many anecdotes that suggest that these intervals are sometimes honoured as much in the breach as in the observance. One friend worked on a pick-your-own strawberry farm that sprayed the fruit with a fungicide against botrytis , or grey-mould, at seven o'clock in the morning then opened to the public for self-pick at ten o'clock. Other friends lived for a time in an apple growing area in England, and when the surrounding orchards were to be sprayed the growers came to their door saying that it was perfectly safe but please would they keep their children indoors, take their washing off the clothes line, keep their pets inside and close all the doors and windows. When the opportunity came they were glad to move back to west Wales!

Bananas are one of the most popular imported fruits and, being soft and easy to eat, large numbers are consumed by children and older people. Unfortunately their high fat content means that they are especially likely to absorb chemical residues, and although they are grown organically in Israel, the Canary Islands and the Caribbean Dominican Republic, the difficulties of transporting them green and then ripening them in the UK without the use of ethylene gas (which is the usual non-organic procedure) means that their availability has been erratic. Organically grown grapes can also be found in season, and they are often distinguished from the conventionally grown fruit by the irregularity of their size, and they usually lack that still life perfection. The usual reason for this cosmetic difference lies in the thinning process. To produce even-shaped and uniformly sized fruit requires careful pruning and thinning, and since this is too labour intensive to be carried out by hand special spray chemicals, or growth regulators, are used instead. These are also used in many apple orchards, and in 1989 there was widespread concern on both sides of the

Atlantic about residues of the growth regulator Alar on apples and apple products that could damage children's health. This affected apple sales, stimulated the development of groups like Parents for Safe Food, and encouraged more growers to turn to organic production.

Seasonal desserts

As the year unfolds, so a sequence of fruits becomes available for cooked desserts. In the spring, rhubarb (though perhaps not strictly a fruit), is the first available and the earliest garden variety, Timperley Early, can usually be pulled from February onwards, whilst in the shops Yorkshire forced rhubarb is sold from the start of the year, or as early as Christmas. However many crumbles we may eat during the season we usually start off with a rhubarb cake as soon as the sticks are large enough to pick. After rhubarb the next candidates for crumble are the gooseberries, first the green varieties, Careless or Leveller, then later the purple Whinhams Industry. (Gooseberries also make a sharp fruit sauce to go with the first summer-caught, rich and oily mackerel). The other treat in late spring/early summer comes when the elder is in blossom. Pick some of the blossom florets, fry them in a thin pancake batter, dust with castor sugar and eat them straight away. These fritters are called *Hollerkuchle* in Franconia, a popular delicacy when the elderflower is in season.

    As the soft fruit ripens, summer pudding with cream or yogurt becomes a first choice, and then later in the summer Barbara celebrates her birthday with Zwetschgenkuchen, a German plum cake (we'd call it a flan). The leaves of scented Geraniums are still young and tender enough at this time of the year to be used in a sorbet, and as the summer draws to its close the most versatile fruit of all, the apple, takes centre stage. Britain is fortunate to have the choice of a large number of culinary apple varieties, many unknown on the continent, and the frothy Bramley and block-shaped Howgate Wonder, for example, are excellent for crumbles or baked whole and stuffed with raisins soaked in grappa.

Barbara uses all the varieties of apples in our orchard to bake apfel strudel in a manner traditional to her family. In her homeland, recipes for apfel strudel vary widely and are handed down from mother to daughter, and families vie to outdo each other with the excellence of their baking. Some recipes call for filo pastry, others for short crust or Danish style puff pastry, whilst the Rottner family recipe uses a thin, light pasta pastry for their inimitable strudel.

From the hedgerows, blackberries make an excellent crumble on their own or with apple; and the bountiful elder produces berries in late autumn which can be used to make a rich and nutritious purée. As each season passes some of the fruits can be stored in a jar and covered in rum, starting with strawberries and ending with plums. By mid-winter the fruit will have fully absorbed the liquor and the resulting rum compote keeps the fruit of the garden desserts going until the first rhubarb is ready to pick once again.

Drinks

One of the great pleasures of foreign travel is to sample local drinks; the wines, beers and spirits, especially those that are difficult to buy at home. In west Wales there's no outstanding regional drink despite the chequered history of local breweries and the existence of that oddity known as Welsh whisky. However, given time the newly planted vineyards of the Teifi Valley may conceivably produce a vintage wine. Still, amongst country people, and this includes newcomers from the city, there's a continuing tradition of wine making and brewing. In the 1970s and 80s the kitchens of the newly arrived organic farmers and gardeners of west Wales seemed full of bubbling demi-johns and bins of home brew, and although the enthusiasm has waned a little, a good proportion of bottles brought to local parties will turn out to be home made wines, and there are some houses where the home brewed beer eclipses anything from large industrial breweries.

One recipe from the country wine repertoire that always rewards with a deliciously fragrant and thirst quenching summer drink is elderflower champagne. This early summer drink is ready in a couple of weeks after bottling, whereas an even quicker spring cocktail can be made by spicing white wine with woodruff to make a 'Maybowl', a perfectly heady drink for sunny evening barbecues and to toast the promise of summer. For the full cocktail add well washed and sliced strawberries to the herb flavoured wine and mix in champagne or a good sparkling wine. As the herbalist Juliette de Baircli Levy reminds us, *"...grape wine is an excellent vehicle for other herbs which may be steeped in it."* It is a wonderful way to keep healthy, and perhaps no coincidence that many traditional after dinner digestive drinks, like Angostura, Underberg, Pastis, Aquavit, Chartreuse, Absinth and Cynar, are made with herbs or from bitter flavoured plants. It is these bitter flavours, now so noticeably absent from modern diets, that stimulate enzymes and aid digestion.

Garden herbs can also be used to make teas which both taste good and have medicinal value. Visitors from Germany are often amazed that the British drink *Schwarzen tee* 'black tea' in the evening, and it is true that the switch to a caffeine and tannin free night cap can promote better sleep. Children enjoy herb teas hot or cold and we also use them exclusively during periods of dieting and fasting. Lemon balm and mint make the most refreshing teas whereas camomile, sage and St John's wort teas are all prescribed by herbalists for particular medicinal uses. The tiny blue flowers of the herb borage, meanwhile, can be picked and frozen in ice cubes to add colour and character to cold drinks and cocktails.

Sloe Gin has a particular place in our affections, and the sight of well berried hedgerows is part of the autumn picture that evokes such an indefinable mixture of serenity and wistfulness. Pleasure, yes, from the mists and mellow fruitfulness, but also a sadness at the passing of summer and some sort of primeval apprehension about the approach of winter.

I first moved to Ty'n yr Helyg one autumn, and when we bought fields surrounding the house (sold from the farm by a previous owner) the sales were always completed in the autumn. The wild harvest from the meadows and the hedges was therefore always the first harvest, and the sloes were abundant each year. By coincidence the house drink at Gasthaus Rottner is *schlehenschnaps*, a sloe Schnapps, and they collect sloes to add whole to the schnapps glass (like olives in a martini), freezing large quantities to keep through the year. Our recipe for sloe gin uses sugar and cinnamon and the liquor gets an extra almondy flavour by crushing the kernels of the sloes in a mortar and pestle, or with a mallet. Sloe gin made in October or early November, before the birds have stripped the bushes, is at its best by Christmas.

Then there's cider. Although west Wales isn't an outstanding apple growing area there are still some years when the local harvest is abundant and by planting appropriate varieties, like the Scottish bred James Grieve, plus a suitable pollinator, even relatively high altitude and exposed gardens will give a reasonable annual crop. And from west Wales the orchards of Hereford are probably more accessible than the valleys of south Wales and the mountains of the north. I've had occasion to visit most of the organic farmers and growers in mid Wales and the border counties, to find many of them restoring and maintaining old cider and perry orchards. It is usually a sideline to the main enterprise, a labour of love. Some cider is made on-farm, and elsewhere fruit is sent to Dunkertons in Pembridge, makers of fine organic cyder and perry. Some years ago the Hereford apple grower Ian Pardoe obtained a press for me, a solid machine of metal and wood. The apples are tipped into a hopper that feeds a hand-turned mill and the pulp falls into the press. Once this is full you screw it down and out pours the juice. We drink the cloudy apple juice fresh, although it will clear if left to stand in a cold place. If left too long, however, the juice starts to ferment and cider or cider vinegar results whether it is wanted or not. News of our press has circulated quite widely and in years when there's a really heavy local apple crop many friends and acquaintances bring along their harvest to make juice to drink fresh, to freeze, or to make apple wine or cider. Although we have no true cider varieties, a blend of dessert and culinary apples and the addition of some crab apples seems to result in a mixture of yeasts and tannins sufficient to produce a very drinkable cider. In fact by varying the proportions of the different varieties it is quite possible to produce a range of sweet and dry ciders, and the addition of a little extra sugar when bottled encourages secondary fermentation, resulting in a sparkling cider – for which you need particularly strong and well-corked bottles. It is at its best from six months to a year after bottling, and to drink a glass of strong sparkling cider brewed from homegrown apples is really to know the meaning of the toast, good health.

Part three

THE FOOD WE EAT

CHAPTER 6

All year round salads

Mixed leaf salad

Use any mixture of leaf salads available according to season. Preferably choose different colours and textures. A short soaking of lettuce in warm water will remove unwanted bitterness. Coarsely chop lettuce or endive with a sharp knife (a blunt knife will bruise the leaves) and soak them in luke warm water. Drain and dry well. Add chopped fresh herbs and toss the mixture in a vinaigrette dressing just prior to serving. Garnish the salad bowl with edible flowers.

Spring salads

Mushroom salad with chives

Choose ¾ lb/350 g button mushrooms that are fresh, firm and small. Wash them thoroughly. Bring a saucepan of water to the boil and tip the mushrooms into the water. Cover the saucepan with a lid. Leave them to blanch for five minutes then strain them through a colander and leave to cool.

Chop some chives very finely. Tip the cooled mushrooms into a bowl, cover with mayonnaise, add the chives and stir well. The bowl can be decorated with sage flowers. When chives are not available, spring onions or red skinned salad onions can be substituted. For garlic mushrooms, use garlic mayonnaise for the dressing.

Mixed beansprouts with rocket and spring onions
Fill a bowl with lukewarm water. Empty 6 oz/175 g of beansprouts into the bowl and wash them well. Skim off the husks with a small sieve or a tea strainer. Tip the cleaned beansprouts into a colander and drain them well. Clean the rocket and spring onions, chop them finely and mix well with the beansprouts.

For a dressing, use olive oil, lemon juice and black pepper or a lemon juice mayonnaise. If rocket is not available, finely chopped radiccio or raw sliced button mushrooms can be used as substitutes.

Alfalfa, mushroom and radish
Use ½ 1b/225 g of alfalfa, ½lb/225 g mushrooms and a bunch of radish. Prepare the salad as for mixed beansprouts. For the dressing, use a blend of sunflower oil, lemon juice, salt and black pepper.

Grated carrot salad
Wash six young carrots and grate them finely. Chop some chervil (or mint or parsley). Mix the grated carrot and the herbs together thoroughly and serve with a mayonnaise or yogurt dressing.

Cooked carrot salad
Wash and dice six medium carrots. Add a sprig of lovage to a pan of salted water and cook the carrots for about five minutes until tender. Drain the carrots and allow to cool; remove the lovage and add an oil and vinegar dressing. Sprinkle the salad with sesame seeds.

Beetroot salad

The most delicious are the small baby beetroots, no more than the size of a tomato.

Boil a dozen baby beetroot in salt water until tender, then drain them and allow to cool. Peel off the skins of the beetroot and slice them finely, but if they are very small they can just be quartered. Use red skinned salad onions, thinly sliced to add to the beetroot.

Make a dressing of oil, vinegar (elderflower vinegar is best), sugar and salt. Pour the dressing over the beetroot and allow to marinate for 2 to 3 hours, or as long as possible.

Welsh onions, spring onions or shallots can be used as a substitute for the red onions.

In the spring, home grown and freshly harvested beetroot leaves can also be used to make a salad. Wash the tender young leaves, then steam them briefly. Cool and garnish with finely chopped chives.

Summer salads

Courgettes and cherry tomatoes

Use green or yellow varieties of courgettes; the yellow varieties, like Goldrush, tend to be sweeter. Choose small, finger sized courgettes wherever possible. Slice one medium sized courgette thinly and halve a pound (450 g) of cherry tomatoes. Chop green or purple basil finely and mix the ingredients well. Toss the salad in a light vinaigrette dressing.

Tomatoes with Little Gem lettuce and marjoram

Chop two Little Gem lettuce and soak in water. Slice half a pound (225 g) of tomatoes. Chop the fresh marjoram and mix the ingredients together well. Toss the salad in a dressing made from lemon juice, oil, salt and black pepper.

A variation on this salad is to use Pak Choi instead of Little Gem.

Fennel and tomato salad

Quarter ½ lb/225 g of tomatoes and let them drain. Halve two medium sized fennel bulbs and cut off and save the green tops for a garnish. Slice the fennel as you would an onion to make rings. Toss the fennel in lemon juice to prevent it browning. Mix together with the tomato and toss in a little olive oil, salt and black pepper.

Cooked fennel salad

Plunge ½ lb/225 g of tomatoes into boiling water for several minutes; this makes them easy to peel. Peel and slice the tomatoes. Slice two medium sized fennel bulbs lengthways (the opposite direction to making rings) and fry briefly on both sides in oil; add a pinch of salt and some black pepper. Leave the fennel to cool, then mix together with the sliced and peeled tomatoes. Serve the dish when fully cold and garnish with the fronds from the fennel tops.

Cucumber with dill and borage flowers

Use ridge cucumbers for preference if they are available; mini cucumbers are also very good.

Slice one cucumber or two mini cucumbers finely and put them in a colander to drain. Slice one red salad onion finely, or finely chop a bunch of spring onions. Chop the fresh dill. Mix a dressing of oil, vinegar, salt and sugar. Mix the cucumber and onions together and pour the dressing over the mixture. Garnish with freshly picked borage flowers.

Crisp lettuce and melon

Home grown melons are likely to be the small sweet Cantaloup variety, but shop bought Honeydew, Ogen or Galia melons will do fine. Mint or lemon balm complements the sweetness of the melon perfectly.

Chop a crisp lettuce finely and soak in warm water, then drain well. Chop the mint or lemon balm. Quarter the melon and spoon out the seeds. Peel the quarters and dice the melon into ¼ inch/½ cm cubes. Mix the ingredients together well and use a yogurt or lemon mayonnaise dressing.

Red lettuce with cucumbers and onion rings

This salad is best with Oak Leaf or Lollo Rosso lettuce, red onions and ridge cucumbers.

Chop the lettuce and soak in warm water, then drain. Slice the cucumber finely and drain. Cut a whole onion into rings, slicing it very finely. Mix the ingredients together and toss well in a dressing of elderflower vinegar, oil and sugar.

For a variation on this salad, simply mix the chopped red lettuce with edible flowers: nasturtium, marigold, sweet rocket, borage and heartsease, then toss in the dressing.

Mixed sweet pepper salad

Choose one each of small yellow, red and green peppers. Cut the peppers into thin strips after removing the stalk and the seeds. Mix the pepper strips with chopped spring onions or a sliced red onion. Dress with oil, salt and lemon juice.

For a variation on this salad, prepare the peppers as above and mix with chopped lettuce. Use a crisp lettuce like Webbs Wonderful, Little Gem hearts or a Batavian lettuce. Chop the lettuce finely, soak in warm water for three minutes, then drain well. Dress as above. For a further variation, substitute celery for the lettuce.

Cooked beans with onions

This recipe is for cooked French dwarf beans, but all kinds of fresh green beans can be used, including young broad beans.

Top and tail ½ lb/225 g of beans and chop into ½ inch/1 cm pieces; or for broad beans, shell from the pods. Bring a pan of water to the boil and add double the normal quantity of salt. Put the beans in the boiling water together with a good sprig of winter savoury, then cook until the beans are tender; this should only take 2 to 3 minutes. To keep the beans a good green colour drain them quickly, then steep them in ice cold water until completely cold. Drain them well. Mix oil, elderflower vinegar, sugar and salt and pour over the beans. Leave to marinate for two or three hours if possible. Chop a red onion finely and sprinkle with black pepper and mix into the salad.

This salad can be made into a more substantial meal by adding ½ lb/225 g peeled and quartered tomatoes or halved cherry tomatoes.

NB Let the prepared tomatoes drain well before adding them to the beans, otherwise they can make the salad too watery.

Autumn salads

Celeriac with land cress or lamb's lettuce

Peel two medium or one large celeriac and cut into slices. Boil in salted water with a teaspoon of lemon juice or vinegar to preserve the white colour of the celeriac. Cook until tender, about 5 to 10 minutes. Drain and leave to cool. Chop a red onion into very fine rings.

Carefully wash and clean the land cress or lamb's lettuce; if using the latter, pay particular attention to the base of the leaves where the matted roots tend to hold the soil. Mix the ingredients together and dress with a mixture of oil, elderflower vinegar and salt.

Leek, apple and walnut salad
Choose one medium or four small leeks. Chop them very finely, then soak in lukewarm water and drain well. Quarter and core two apples and slice thinly. Crisp red skinned apples are best. Soak them in lemon juice to stop them browning. Chop a handful of walnuts into small pieces. Mix all the ingredients together. Toss the salad in a vinaigrette dressing just prior to serving.

Chinese cabbage with mizuna and orange
Chop half a Chinese cabbage and a bunch of mizuna finely; soak in lukewarm water, then drain well. Peel and quarter an orange, then slice the quarters finely. Drain, then mix the ingredients together. Toss the salad in a yogurt or lemon and oil dressing.

For variations on this salad, grapes or grapefruit can be used instead of the orange. The grapes should be washed and halved before using. Grapefruits, especially the pink fleshed Ruby Red grapefruit, are an excellent substitute for either orange or grapes. They need to be peeled, quartered and then sliced thinly before mixing with the other ingredients.

Endive, radiccio and pineapple
Either frisée endive or the broad leaved variety can be used in this salad.

Chop the endive finely, cut the radiccio in half and slice very finely into long thin strips. Soak both in warm water. Drain well. Peel and core the pineapple (ie cut out the stem). Chop into small cubes and mix with the endive and radiccio. Toss in a yogurt or lemon and oil dressing. Sliced orange can be used as a substitute for the pineapple.

Celery, carrot and pepper salad
Use one stick of celery, one green pepper and two medium sized carrots. Chop the celery finely, soak in warm water for three minutes, then drain well. Halve and clean the pepper, removing all of the seeds and cut into fine long strips. Peel the carrot and cut into thin slices; rinse them well. Add one ounce of finely chopped wild celery leaves or parsley (preferably broad leaved parsley). Mix the ingredients together well and toss in yogurt dressing or vinaigrette.

Winter salads

White cabbage and mizuna
Quarter the cabbage and grate it finely. Chop the mizuna finely. Mix well and dress with mayonnaise or lemon mayonnaise. If available, decorate the salad with chive flowers or marigold petals. Parsley makes an excellent substitute for the mizuna.

Cabbage salad with hot dressing
Proceed as above but use parsley, not mizuna. Chop streaky bacon into small cubes and fry until completely crisp. While still hot, pour the bacon and the hot fat over the cabbage and mix well. Add a small amount of the following dressing: oil, vinegar, sugar, salt and ground black pepper.

Red cabbage and pear
Red cabbage stores very well, and like hard white cabbage it is available throughout the winter.
    Quarter the red cabbage and remove the inner stalk. Grate the cabbage finely. Quarter and slice a pear and soak in lemon juice to prevent it browning in the salad. Mix the pear and cabbage together and serve with a yogurt dressing. Chopped walnuts can be added to this salad.

Chicory and orange

Halve the chicory and remove the base which tends to be very bitter. Slice the chicory finely and put in lukewarm water for three minutes. Drain well. While the chicory is draining peel, slice and cube an orange. To add some colour, roughly chop one of the following: parsley, watercress, rocket or lamb's lettuce; or, if available, sprouted sunflower seeds. Put the chicory, orange and green garnish together in a bowl and mix well. Make a dressing of lemon juice, sunflower oil, salt and black pepper. Add the dressing to the salad just before serving to preserve the crispness of the chicory.

Calabrese, cauliflower and clementines

Use one small cauliflower or half a large one, two clementines and half a pound (225 g) of calabrese. Wash and chop the cauliflower and calabrese into florets. Peel two clementines or one orange and divide into segments. Mix the ingredients together well and dress with a vinaigrette or yogurt dressing.

Cooked cauliflower salad

Wash and chop one small cauliflower or half a large one. Cook in salted water until tender, about five to ten minutes. Drain the cauliflower and cool. Toss in a yogurt dressing with freshly ground black pepper and finely chopped parsley.

Salad dressings

Vinaigrette
½ pint/275 ml stock
1½ tablespoons mustard
2 tablespoons brown sugar
¼ pint/150 ml white wine vinegar
1 teaspoon salt
¾ pint/425 ml sunflower oil

Blend together the brown sugar, salt and mustard. To this mixture add the vinegar. At this point it should be strong tasting as the stock is mixed in at the end to thin the vinaigrette down. Mix in the sunflower oil and blend well to a mayonnaise-like consistency. Add the stock and stir well. This is a basic vinaigrette dressing and we modify it, using different herb or fruit vinegars, depending on the particular salad to be dressed. The vinaigrette will keep for several weeks in an airtight container in a cool place. Always stir it well before using.

Yogurt

Yogurt dressing is a favourite with weight watchers and it evokes memories of salads from Greece and the eastern Mediterranean. Although the Mediterranean recipes traditionally used goat or ewe's milk yogurt, we use the milder flavoured cow's milk yogurt from Rachel's Dairy, or you can start by making your own yogurt.

Home made yogurt
1 pint/570 ml milk
small carton live natural yogurt

Bring the milk to the boil and allow to simmer for 1 minute. Let the milk cool to between 98.4°F and 100°F (37– 40°C). Take a tablespoon of the live yogurt and put it in a bowl. Stir in the cooled milk and mix thoroughly. Cover the bowl tightly with muslin or a plastic bag and leave overnight in a warm place where the temperature will remain constant – like the airing cupboard or by the Rayburn. Ideally use a vacuum flask and leave the mixture for at least eight hours. This method just about always works although the consistency of the yogurt is rather variable. If you really want a thick yogurt, you can cheat a bit by adding powdered milk until you get the required consistency.

Yogurt dressing
1 tablespoon stock
1 pot Rachel's Dairy low fat yogurt
salt
chopped parsley, chervil, chive or mint

Stir the stock into the yogurt. Add salt to taste and add the chopped herb for flavour and decoration.

Sweet and savoury mayonnaise

2 eggs

½ pint/275 ml sunflower oil

1 tablespoon white wine vinegar

½ teaspoon salt

½ tablespoon sugar

1½ tablespoons Welsh wholegrain
   mustard

1 pot Rachel's Dairy low fat yogurt

Break the eggs into a blender and whisk until foaming and nearly white. Slowly pour in the oil with the blender still whisking. Add the vinegar, using only a small quantity for flavouring. Now add the salt, sugar and mustard. Whisk it all together in the blender and thin to the desired consistency with the yogurt. If kept covered, or in a screw-topped jar, the mayonnaise will keep for several days in a refrigerator.

Garlic mayonnaise

2 eggs

½ pint/275 ml sunflower oil or cold-pressed grape seed oil

2 tablespoons German delicatessen mustard

½ tablespoon salt

juice of two lemons

3 large cloves garlic

1 pot Rachel's Dairy low fat yogurt

Put the eggs in a blender and whisk until foaming and nearly white. Slowly add in the oil. Add the mustard, salt and the lemon juice. Crush the garlic cloves, add them to the mixture and whisk it all together in the blender. Thin with the yogurt.

Lemon mayonnaise
2 eggs
½ pint/275 ml sunflower oil or cold-pressed grape seed oil
1 tablespoon German delicatessen mustard
1 tablespoon salt
juice of two lemons
1 pot Rachel's Dairy low fat yogurt

Whisk the eggs in a blender until foaming and nearly white. Slowly add the oil with the blender still whisking. Add the mustard, salt and lemon juice and whisk them all together. Thin to the desired consistency with the yogurt.

Tofu vegetarian mayonnaise
1 pack or ¼ lb/110 g tofu
¼ pint/150 ml olive oil
¼ pint/150 ml white wine vinegar
½ teaspoon dill
1 teaspoon honey

Whisk the tofu in a blender. Add the oil slowly, then the seasoning, vinegar and honey. Adjust the honey and seasoning to taste. Caraway seed can be used instead of dill if the mayonnaise is to be used to bind coleslaw, and tarragon can be substituted when the mayonnaise is used to dress cold cooked vegetables.

Tahini dressing
1 tablespoon plain yogurt
2 tablespoons light tahini
juice of one lemon
garlic salt and black pepper
chopped chives
lovage

Combine the garlic salt and black pepper with the lemon juice, then blend in the yogurt and the tahini. This is a good substitute for mayonnaise with new potatoes. Sprinkle with chopped chives and lovage.

Lemon and oil dressing
juice of two lemons
½ pint/275 ml sunflower oil or cold-pressed grape seed oil or olive oil
1 tablespoon salt
freshly ground black pepper

Mix the lemon juice and the oil together with the salt and the pepper. Add the dressing to the salad just before serving to preserve the crispness. For some particularly strongly flavoured salads, such as those with rocket and spring onions, olive oil can be used in preference to the milder sunflower or grape seed oils.

Asparagus

bunch of asparagus (about 1 lb/450 g)
salt
2 oz/50 g melted butter (to dress the hot dish) or white wine vinegar, salt and
sunflower oil (for a salad dressing)

Peel the lower stems of the asparagus and place them upright in a pan of warm
water so they are nearly submerged. Add salt and cook until tender (this will
depend on the thickness of the stems). Drain the asparagus and reserve the water
to make soup and/or a salad dressing. Either serve the asparagus hot
with a simple sauce of melted butter, or cold as a salad.

For the salad, make a dressing using some of the reserved water from
cooking and, in the words of Barbara's mother, add, *"essig wie ein Geizhls, Salz wie
ein Weiser, Ol wie ein Verschwender"* ("vinegar like a miser, salt like a sage, and oil
like lady bountiful").

Soup recipes

Asparagus soup
water preserved from cooking asparagus
2 oz/50 g butter
1 oz/25 g flour
small pot of cream
salt and pepper (preferably cayenne pepper)
glass of white wine
juice of 1 lemon

Mix the flour with half of the butter, then combine the mixture with the asparagus water. Add the cream, then strain the soup through a fine sieve. Mix in the white wine and the lemon juice. Season with salt and pepper to taste. Heat the soup and, just before serving, mix in the rest of the cold butter.

Herb soup
1 small onion, finely chopped
2 small potatoes, chopped small
2 oz/50 g chervil
1 oz/25 g parsley
sprig of lemon balm or small bunch of chives
salt and pepper

juice of 1 lemon
2 cups water
1 glass white wine
½ teaspoon brown sugar
2 oz/50 g butter
small pot of cream

Fry the onions and the potatoes, then add two-thirds of the finely chopped herbs and the water. Add salt, pepper, lemon juice and brown sugar to taste. Bring the mixture to the boil and simmer gently for a few minutes. During cooking, the potatoes thicken the soup, and they are used in preference to flour for this purpose. Liquidize then strain. Season with white wine and cream. As the herbs tend to go grey when cooked in the soup, keep back a third of the chopped herbs and combine them with 2 oz/50 g of butter to make a herb butter. Just before serving, add the dark green herb butter and whisk it well. This both gives the herb soup a better colour and helps to thicken it.

Chervil Soup
2 shallots or small onions
2 medium sized potatoes
1 oz/25 g butter for frying
1 oz/25 g softened butter
glass of white wine
small tot of Pernod (or any other pastis)
large bunch of fresh chervil (in fact as much as possible), finely chopped
2 pints/1.14L stock (preferably beef stock)
small pot of cream
salt and pepper

Peel and slice the potatoes and onions and cook them in butter until the onions become transparent. Add the wine and the Pernod, most of the chopped chervil (but save some to add at the end) and the stock. Bring to the boil and simmer gently until the potatoes are soft. Strain the mixture through a sieve, purée the solids, then return them to the liquid. Add the cream and season to taste. While the soup is re-heating, mix the softened butter with the remaining chervil and fold this into the soup prior to serving. The chervil butter enhances the fresh chervil taste and gives the soup a good bright green colour.

Sorrel soup
½ lb/225 g sorrel
2 small potatoes, chopped very small
1 small onion
¼ pint/150 ml milk
glass of white wine
salt, sugar, pepper
2 oz/50 g butter
pot of plain 'B & A' yogurt
parsley or chives

Chop the onion finely and fry until transparent. Mix in the potatoes and add two-thirds of the well washed and roughly chopped sorrel. Fry briefly, then cover the sorrel with water. Simmer for 5 minutes and add salt, pepper and sugar to taste. The potatoes will break up and thicken the soup and they are used in preference to flour for this purpose. Add the milk, then liquidize the soup and add the wine. The remaining sorrel leaves should be finely chopped and mixed with the butter and formed into small balls. Just before serving, stir in the sorrel butter balls to give the soup an extra green colour and to give it extra creaminess. Top the soup with the yogurt, which is an excellent substitute for soured cream, and serve sprinkled with finely chopped parsley or chives.

Salads with fish

Carp with lamb's lettuce and celeriac
1 fresh carp
1 pint/570 ml beer
l oz/25 g butter
salt, pepper and paprika
flour, for coating
for the salads
l lb/450 g celeriac
2 red skinned onions
¼ lb/110 g lamb's lettuce
vinegar, oil
salt, sugar, black pepper
lemon juice

Halve and clean the carp, then marinate for a good 15 minutes in beer. Salt both sides of the carp halves, then spice with pepper and sweet paprika. Turn them in flour and bake at 160°C in the oven, basting them with a good tablespoon of butter until they are an even golden brown. Melt another tablespoon of butter in a frying pan and toss the carp in the hot fat just before serving.

To make the salad, peel and slice the celeriac and cook in salted water with a dessertspoon of vinegar or lemon juice to retain the white colour. Drain the cooked celeriac and while still warm, toss in a mixture of vinegar (elderflower or borage vinegar is best), oil, salt and sugar. Add freshly ground black pepper and thinly sliced onion. Mix together well. Wash the lamb's lettuce thoroughly, then soak in warm water. Drain well and mix with lemon juice, oil and salt. Serve the celeriac and the lamb's lettuce salads separately with the carp.

Baked sewin

Sewin, or sea trout, is the great delicacy of the game rivers of west Wales and the local anglers' greatest prize. When in season, from March to October, the freshly caught fish is available in local shops. Leave the fish whole, simply gut it and wash well. Rub with salt inside and out. Fill the inside of the fish with fresh herbs. Ideally use fresh dill. Fennel or a mixture of any garden herbs such as sorrel, lemon balm or parsley will do. Wrap the fish in foil and bake in a slow oven for half an hour.

Serve the sewin on a bed of purslane with boiled potatoes and a fresh leaf salad.

Potatoes

Potato salad
3 lbs/1½ kg potatoes
chives or parsley
vinaigrette dressing
sweet and savoury mayonnaise

Wash the potatoes but do not peel them. Depending on their size, halve or quarter the potatoes and boil them in salted water, then drain. Leave them until cool enough to handle. Peel the still warm potatoes (they peel easiest when still warm) then set aside to cool completely before slicing.

Slice the potatoes thinly and add finely chopped chives or parsley to taste. Add a generous amount of vinaigrette dressing and leave to soak for two hours, or if possible overnight. The vinaigrette can be mixed with sweet and savoury mayonnaise for a very rich potato salad.

Potato salad with hot dressing
3 lbs/1½ potatoes
chives or parsley
3 rashers Welsh organic bacon

for the dressing
1 tablespoon wine vinegar
5 tablespoons oil
sugar, salt and black pepper

Cook and slice the potatoes as above and mix with the parsley or chives. Chop three rashers of streaky bacon into small cubes and fry until completely crisp. While still hot, pour the cubes of bacon and the fat over the potatoes and mix in well. Add a small amount of oil and vinegar mixed with salt and sugar. Add ground black pepper.

Papas arrugadas (wrinkly potatoes)
This recipe is the one used by Riccardo Orlando at Puntazzo Restaurant in
Ginostra; he adopted it after a visit to Lanzarote.

4½ lb/2 kg small potatoes; firm waxy varieties are best
18 oz/½ kg sea salt
enough water to cover the potatoes

Boil the potatoes whole in their jackets until they fall off a skewer or knife, say
20 minutes. Drain the potatoes but don't peel them. Cut the potatoes in half and
arrange them cut surfaces upwards on a plate. If you've used kidney shaped or
oval potatoes, then you can make the shape of a butterfly. Serve them with
mayonnaise, garlic mayonnaise, or simply with butter.

   This recipe calls for a lot of potatoes and it's good for a dinner party or
barbecue. It's important to use a lot of salt and vital not to cut the potato skins or
else the potatoes will absorb the salt and become inedible. If you scale down the
quantity of potatoes, then reduce the amount of salt in proportion.

Roest kartoffel (pan fried potatoes)
3 lbs/1½ kg potatoes
1 large onion
3 rashers Welsh organic bacon
small bunch of parsley
½ teaspoon caraway seeds

Use left-over potatoes, or if not available, boil the potatoes and let them cool.
Slice them. Fry the onion and finely chopped bacon, then add in the cold, sliced
potatoes. Spice with caraway seeds and chopped parsley.

   Eat the *Roest kartoffel* with *bratwurst* (spicy wholemeat pork sausages), grilled
or fried meat, or with omelette and green salad.

Kartoffel knoedel (potato dumplings)
There are many kinds of potato dumplings which are traditional specialities of Franconia and recipes vary from village to village. The two most common are *Rohe knoedel* made from grated raw potato, and *Gekocht knoedel* made from mashed potato with egg and cornflour. They are usually served with roast pork, or beef, and with lots of gravy.

Rohe knoedel
4 lbs/2 kg potatoes
4 pints salted water
a good pinch of salt
2 stale bread rolls
1½ oz/40 g fat

Peel all the potatoes, then divide them into two halves. Slice half of them, cover with salted water and cook until the potatoes are soft. Wash them and keep them warm. Take the other half of the potatoes and grate them finely into a bowl of salted water (if you don't do this, the grated potatoes will turn brown). When all the potatoes are grated, strain them through a muslin cloth and squeeze hard to dry them. After the water has been expelled, some starchy pulp will come through the cloth. This should be saved and mixed back into the dough later. Mix the grated potato together with the warm mashed potato, salt to taste and stir it to make a dough. Dice the stale bread rolls and fry the cubes in the fat as if you were making croûtons; these are then used to stuff the dumplings. First mould the potato dough into round dumplings, then fill them with the fried bread cubes. Cook the dumplings in salted water for 30 minutes with the lid firmly on the pan. Serve immediately.

Gekochte knoedel
1½lbs/700 g cooked (boiled) potatoes
3 oz/75 g flour
3 oz/75 g cornflour
2 tablespoons milk
2 eggs
salt, marjoram
1 stale bread roll
1 oz/25 g butter

These dumplings are usually made with potatoes left over from the day before. Grate the cooked potatoes finely and mix them into a dough with the flour, cornflour, milk, eggs, salt and marjoram. Dice the stale bread roll and fry the cubes in butter as if making croûtons; these are used to stuff the dumplings. Mould the potato and flour dough into dumpling shapes and fill them with the fried bread cubes. Simmer the dumplings very gently for 15 to 20 minutes in salted water.

When they are done, they float to the surface. Serve immediately. In the autumn, it's traditional to eat these dumplings with roast pigeon.

Breads and baking

Wheat flour recipe for rolls and loaves
For this recipe you need to prepare three bowls:

Bowl 1 – the flour
2 lb/900 g flour – use one-third white organic unbleached flour and two-thirds organic brown flour. Depending on the kind of bread you like, the proportions of white and brown flour can be varied. Mix the flours together and add a handful of caraway, poppy or sesame seeds.

Bowl 2 – the yeast
To raise this flour you need:
1 tablespoon dried yeast
1 teaspoon brown sugar or honey
½ pint/275 ml warm water
Mix the yeast, sugar or honey and warm water, leave in a warm place to rise until it becomes very frothy.

Bowl 3 – water and oil
To make the dough you also need:
½ pint/275 ml hot water
2 heaped teaspoons sea salt
1 teaspoon oil (eg sunflower oil)
1 teaspoon brown sugar or honey
Mix these ingredients together and add a little cold water until the mixture is warm rather than hot. (If the water is too hot it will kill the yeast.)

Now combine the contents of bowls 2 and 3, and mix together. Pour this mixture into the bowl containing the flour. Knead thoroughly until firm and smooth. To get the right texture, it may be necessary to add either a little extra flour, if the dough is too moist, or some lukewarm water, if it's too stiff. Different types of flour absorb more or less water so it's difficult to be exact about this, and it will depend on the actual proportions of different flours used.

To make a light bread it's vital now to let the dough rise by leaving it in a warm place covered with a damp cloth.

When the dough has risen, it should be knocked back, ie kneaded again. In order to make a crust, the dough should either be rolled in oats or kneaded finally in coarse brown flour.

To make loaves

Form the dough into loaf shapes and place in baking tins and leave to prove (rise). When the dough has risen in the tins, bake the loaves in a hot oven until golden brown; this will take about 20 minutes. Now switch off the oven; tip the loaves out of the tins, turn them upside down, replace them in the oven and leave until the oven is cool.

To make rolls

Roll the dough out until about one inch thick. To form the rolls, use a biscuit cutter and press out the shapes as if you were making jam tarts. The size of cutter entirely depends on the size of rolls you want. Place the rolls on an oiled tray and leave to prove. Bake them in a very hot oven until golden brown; about ten minutes is usually enough. Remove the rolls from the tray and leave them to cool in a basket or on a wire rack. Rolls and loaves that aren't going to be used straight away can be frozen, so it's worth baking large batches for a week's supply. Put one loaf or half a dozen rolls in a plastic bag to prevent freezer blast, seal the bag or tie it securely and freeze straight away.

Rye bread

Sourdough ryebread is made without yeast, and the first step in its preparation is to make a 'starter' to raise the ryedough. The recipe for ryebread looks complicated; in fact it is quite straightforward but involves a number of steps over a twenty-four hour period. In this recipe, we have assumed that you start to make the bread at eleven o'clock in the morning, but of course the schedule can be planned for whatever time is most suitable.

The 'starter'

You need to start the 'starter' four days before making the bread, but this only needs to be done once since some of the dough from each batch of ryebread making can be put aside to be used next time as the 'starter'.

Use a wooden or plastic bowl, but not a metal one and mix ¼ pint/150 ml of lukewarm water with some ryeflour until it has a thin and smooth paste-like consistency. The amount of ryeflour needed to make the paste depends very much on the texture and quality of the flour – it varies considerably.

To get the sourdough 'starter' to ferment, you now add some buttermilk and a pinch of caraway seed, then leave the covered bowl in a warm place for three days. The starter should ferment and start to bubble. On the evening of the third day, add some more water and flour until you get a porridge-like consistency. Cover the bowl again and leave overnight in a warm place.

Ryebread loaves

Day 1 – 11am Take 2 oz/50 g of the starter dough and mix with 2 fl oz of lukewarm water. Cover with a cloth and leave in a warm place for one hour.

12 noon Now add 4 fl oz/110 ml of lukewarm water and mix it with enough ryeflour to make a porridge-like consistency. Cover again with a cloth and leave in a warm place for eight hours.

8 pm Add a further 8 fl oz/225 ml of lukewarm water and mix with more ryeflour to make a slightly stiffer dough. Cover and leave until the next morning.

Day 2 – 8am Add another 8 fl oz/225 ml of lukewarm water and mix with enough ryeflour to make a porridge-like consistency. Cover and leave.

12 noon Take away 1oz/25 g of the dough to keep as a starter for next time. Knead the saved dough with a little ryeflour until stiff and wrap it in cling film. Keep it in the 'fridge.

To the remaining dough, add 22 fl oz/625 ml of lukewarm water and mix well. Add ½ oz/15 g of salt, 4 tablespoons of wheat flour and a handful of caraway seeds. Fennel seeds or sunflower seeds can be used as a substitute according to taste. For a bread to aid digestion and to ease constipation use linseed instead. Now mix with enough ryeflour to form a stiff dough, then form the dough into two round loaves. Dust the loaves with flour and place on a lightly-floured baking tray and leave to rise for one hour.

Brush the loaves with water and put them in a pre-heated oven (220°C). Bake the loaves for one hour or until you see that a dark crust has formed. At this point, brush the loaves with water again and shortly after, switch off the oven and leave the loaves inside to cool.

This bread keeps well and is best enjoyed a day or two after baking.

Stöllen
3 lb/1.4 kg flour
1 pint/570 ml milk
4 oz/110 g yeast
1 whole egg
2 egg yolks
½ oz/15 g salt
7 oz/200 g sugar
11 oz/315 g margarine
4 oz/110 g candied lemon
3 oz/75 g candied orange
1½ lb/700 g sultanas
rind of 1 lemon
4 oz/110 g chopped almonds
rum or cherry or plum liqueur

Allow the yeast to rise by putting it in a bowl with a quarter of the milk and a spoonful of the sugar. Leave it in a warm place. Once it's risen, mix in the flour to make a bread-like dough. Stir in all the other ingredients, then knead until the dough falls easily from your hands. Form the dough into long loaf-shaped cakes and leave to rise for 30 minutes. Bake in a hot oven until golden brown. Leave the stöllen to cool, then wrap them in a tea-cloth or in linen to prevent them drying out and leave to mature for a week or so. During the Christmas season bring them out, dust with icing sugar, and serve sliced like a fruit bread.

Apfel Strudel

for the pastry
9 oz/250 g flour
1 whole egg
1 egg yolk
2½ oz/60 g melted butter
1 tablespoon cooking oil
1 teaspoon vinegar
1 cup warm water
pinch salt
1 teaspoon sugar
for the filling
1½ peeled, cored and chopped apples
2 oz/50 g raisins
cinnamon
2 oz/50 g sugar (or to taste)

Mix the pastry ingredients together and knead it till shining and smooth. Roll out very thinly and cover with the apples, raisins, cinnamon and sugar. Roll the strudel into a cylinder, seal the ends and place on a baking tray. Bake in a hot oven for 20 to 30 minutes, occasionally removing it to pour some milk over the strudel (once or twice should be sufficient).

Pickles and sauces

Mojo Palmero

The green dips served with meals in El Hierro and La Palma are delicious. They are made from capsicums and almonds, and in one version, coriander is used instead of capsicums.

12 dried peppers
2 large bulbs of garlic
almonds
olive oil
cumin
salt and a little wine vinegar

In this version, the peppers are soaked the previous day, then they are mixed into a paste with the other ingredients. Traditionally this was done in a wooden mortar; today a food mixer is used.

Green mojo

This was the version we most enjoyed and is a wonderful bright green colour. The recipe is the same as for *Mojo Palmero* but green capsicums replace the dried ones. This green mojo doesn't keep and should be used the day it is made.

Coriander mojo

Use the same recipe but here the peppers are replaced by fresh coriander.

Cucumber pickle (bread and butter pickle)
3 large or 6 ridge or mini cucumbers
4 onions, skinned and sliced
3 tablespoons salt
¾ pint/425 ml white wine vinegar
5 oz/150 g sugar
1 teaspoon celery seeds
1 teaspoon black mustard seeds

Slice the cucumbers very thinly and layer them in a bowl with the sliced onion; sprinkle each layer with salt. Leave for an hour, then rinse and drain well.

Put the sugar, vinegar, celery and mustard seeds in a saucepan and heat until the sugar is dissolved, then simmer for three minutes. Finally pack the cucumber mixture into preheated jars and add enough of the vinegar liquid to cover. Seal the jars immediately with an airtight lid. Store the pickle in a dark place to preserve the colour of the cucumber. The pickle will mature for two months and then be ready to eat.

Fruit and desserts

Fruit salad

Melon, banana and orange are the all year round basis of fruit salad to which, each season, fresh fruit can be added. In summer peach, blackcurrants, strawberry and raspberry are added; in autumn blackberries, plums and grapes are in season.

The fruit should be washed, peeled and chopped as required then strained through a colander. Sugar can be added according to taste and sunflower seeds add an extra dimension. Cream or Greek style yogurt finishes off the fruit salad.

Rhubarb cake

4 oz/110 g sugar
8 oz/225 g butter or margarine
12 oz/350 g flour
1 egg
pinch of salt
pinch of cinnamon
rind of 1 lemon, grated
1 teaspoon baking powder
for the filling
6 stems of rhubarb, peeled and finely chopped
1 teaspoon cinnamon
2 tablespoons brown sugar

Mix the butter, sugar and egg and beat to a smooth paste, then add the grated lemon peel. Add the flour, baking powder, cinnamon and salt and knead until a even consistency. Roll out the pastry and line a flan or tart tray. Cover the tray with the rhubarb and sprinkle with a mixture of sugar and cinnamon. Bake in hot oven for 20 to 30 minutes, until the fruit is cooked and the pastry is a golden brown.

The flan base of the Rhubarb cake (page163) can be used for a successful fruit tart throughout the seasons, eg for:

Zwetschgen kuchen (plum flan)
Line the flan base with halves of de-stoned plums and sprinkle with the sugar and cinnamon mixture.

Apple flan
Peel 2 large or 4 small cooking apples. Quarter them, remove the core and cut into slices. Line the flan base, sprinkle with sugar and cinnamon and add a handful of raisins before baking.

Hollerkuchle (elderflower fritters)
10 –12 elderflower heads
½lb/225 g flour
2 eggs
½ pint/275 ml milk
pinch of salt
oil or lard for frying
castor sugar and cinnamon

Wash the flower heads and drain them well. Make a batter by mixing the flour with the eggs, milk and salt. Turn the flower heads in the batter and deep-fry in hot cooking oil or lard. Remove from the fat and place them on greaseproof paper. Sprinkle with sugar and cinnamon and eat them straight away while still hot.

Cherry fritters with sage leaves
1 pint/570 ml milk
2 eggs
4 egg whites
11 oz/315 g flour
pinch salt
1 lb/450 g cherries (de-stoned)
large bunch of fresh sage leaves
margarine or lard for frying
icing sugar
vanilla ice cream

Mix together the milk, eggs, egg whites, flour and salt and beat to the consistency of a thick paste. Heat the fat in a pan, then add the cherries to the fritter mixture. Spoon the coated cherries into the hot fat, using five or six cherries to make one fritter. Spoon some of the hot fat over the fritters so that they rise well. Fry until golden brown and dust with icing sugar.

Take the sage leaves one at a time, dip them in the fritter mixture so that they are well coated, then fry in the hot fat. Dust them with icing sugar, then arrange them on a plate with the cherry fritters and serve with vanilla ice cream.

Rhubarb sorbet

4 good stems of rhubarb, peeled and chopped (keep the peel)
1 glass white wine
4 oz/110 g sugar
¼ pint/150 ml water
1 teaspoon cinnamon
juice of a lemon
drop of champagne or sparkling white wine

Cook the rhubarb peelings with the white wine, water, and half of the sugar and cinnamon. Reduce to a syrup.

Strain the liquid, add the chopped rhubarb and cook until tender. Whisk the mixture to a purée, then strain if preferred. Otherwise, just add the rest of the sugar, cinnamon and the lemon juice but be careful not to make it too sweet. Add a few drops of champagne or sparkling white wine, transfer to a suitable container and place in the freezer. Leave for at least an hour, but now and then bring it out and stir gently so that the sorbet freezes evenly.

Geranium sorbet

12 leaves of scented geranium (lemon or rose)

4 oz/110 g sugar

¼ pint/150 ml water

juice of a large lemon

1 egg white

Bring the water to the boil and dissolve the sugar. Remove from heat and add the geranium leaves, then steep for 30 minutes. (If the flavour seems too weak, bring the liquid to the boil again and leave for a further 15 minutes). Strain the syrup into a suitable container, add the lemon juice and leave to stand until cool. Put the container into the freezer for 45 to 60 minutes until the syrup is partially frozen. Whisk the egg white to a snow and fold into the sorbet. Return to the freezer until hard (this should take about an hour). Serve the sorbet in drinking glasses decorated with fresh leaves.

Mint Sorbet

Follow the above recipe but use mint leaves. Peppermint or applemint are best.

Kaiserschmarrn (emperor's waffle)
4 eggs
1 oz/25 g sugar
½ pint/275 ml milk
4½ oz/130 g flour
pinch of salt
1 oz/25 g sultanas or raisins
2 oz/50 g butter (or cooking oil)
icing sugar

Mix together the sugar, salt and egg yolks, then beat in the milk and flour until you have the consistency of thick, pouring cream. Add the sultanas and raisins. Whisk the egg whites to a snow, then fold them into the mixture. Heat the butter or oil in a pan, then pour in the mixture; fry gently turning over to crisp both sides. Transfer to an oven (200°C) and bake until golden brown (10 to 15 minutes). Remove from the oven, break into small pieces, then leave to steam for several minutes. Serve hot, dusted with icing sugar.

Recipes for drinks

Elderflower champagne
1 gallon/4½ L cold water
1¼lb/560 g sugar
7 elderflower heads
2 lemons
2 tablespoons white wine vinegar or cider vinegar

Bring the water to the boil and pour it over the sugar. When the sugar has dissolved, allow the solution to cool. Slice the lemons, then add the flower heads, lemon slices and the vinegar. Cover and leave to stand for 24 hours. Strain off the liquid and siphon off into bottles. Use strong bottles and cork well as this wine is very fizzy.
Note: Elderberries are very rich in vitamin C; in September pick the berries before the birds strip the trees and make a thick syrup which can be used as a base for a warming, fortifying punch during the winter. Elderberries also make a good country wine, and in Austria they are used to colour pale red grape wine.

May Bowl
Pick a large bunch of woodruff from the garden just before it flowers. Tie the woodruff in a tight bunch. Pour a bottle of dry white wine into a bowl or a decanter with a wide rim. Suspend the bunch of woodruff upside down so that it's completely submerged in the wine, but don't let the cut stems of the plant into the wine or else the sap will spoil the flavour. Leave to steep for several hours, then remove the woodruff. Add well-washed and sliced strawberries, chill and, before serving, mix in champagne or a good sparkling white wine.

Sloe gin
1½ lb/700 g sloes
12 oz/350 g sugar
1 stick cinnamon
1 bottle gin

Check through the sloes, discard any that are not sound and wash them well. Crush the sloes either in a pestle with a mortar, or in a dish-cloth with a wooden mallet. Put the crushed fruit, together with the sugar and cinnamon, into a jar and then pour the gin over the mixture. Fit a lid to the jar and screw down tight, then leave to marinate for at least a month. To bottle the sloe gin, strain the mixture through muslin or a fine sieve, then it's ready to drink.

Puntazzo recipes

Pasta with sweet peppers
4 large red peppers
8 fl oz/225 ml extra virgin olive oil
3 cloves garlic, crushed
1 tablespoon salt

Cook the large fleshy red peppers over an open flame, or under a grill, until they are entirely blackened. Remove them from the heat, then rub them on kitchen paper to remove the charred skins. This can be done quickly with water under the tap, but the smokiness in the flavour is then lost. Cut the peppers open and remove the seeds. Slice them into very thin strips. Finally marinate in the extra virgin olive oil, garlic and salt. The sauce is served with spaghetti and sprinkled with a little grated Parmesan cheese. At Puntazzo, they recommend the Sicilian wine Cellaro Bianco with this dish.

Hot wine sauce

1 lemon

4 tablespoons olive oil

1 large onion, chopped

4 fl oz/110 ml dry white wine

1 tablespoon salt

1 tablespoon freshly ground black pepper

2 oz/50 g chopped parsley

Peel and dice the lemon, taking care to remove all the pith and skin. Heat the oil and fry the onion. Add the prepared lemon and the wine (at Puntazzo, Riccardo uses Vermentino, a white wine from Sardinia) and a seasoning of salt and pepper. Reduce the sauce over a high heat for about 5 minutes. Add the chopped parsley at the last moment. Serve immediately. It is excellent with grilled or barbecued fish.

Polpette di Melanzane (aubergine croquettes)
½ lb/225 g aubergines, peeled and cut into 1 inch slices
1 tablespoon salt
1 egg
3 oz/75 g freshly grated Parmesan
2 garlic cloves, crushed
1 oz/25 g fresh basil leaves
2 oz/50 g fresh breadcrumbs
8 fl oz/225 ml oil

Bring a pan of water to the boil and place the aubergines in it. Add the salt and cook for 10 to 15 minutes, taking care not to over-cook them. When ready, drain them and place under a weighted board to remove as much water as possible.

As soon as they are cool enough to handle, mash them by hand and work in the egg, Parmesan, garlic and chopped basil. Add enough breadcrumbs to make the mixture firm.

Heat the oil in a large saucepan. Use a tablespoon to drop scoops of the mixture into the oil. Turn the croquettes over gently as soon as they are done on one side. When they are evenly browned on each side, drain them on kitchen paper.

These croquettes can be eaten hot or cold. The recommended wine is Forastera, a white wine from Ischia.

Pasta with fresh vegetable sauce

6 ripe tomatoes, seeded and chopped (or a tin of Italian plum tomatoes)

1 yellow pepper, seeded and chopped

2 cloves garlic, finely chopped

4 oz/110 g capers, chopped

1 celery heart, chopped

4 tablespoons extra virgin olive oil

1 teaspoon cayenne pepper

½ teaspoon salt

8 oz/225 g freshly grated Parmesan or Pecorino cheese

Combine the chopped vegetables thoroughly. Transfer them to an earthenware bowl and cover with the extra virgin olive oil. Season with cayenne pepper and salt and leave to marinate for at least two hours.

This sauce can be eaten with any kind of pasta. Sprinkle the dish lavishly with grated Parmesan or Pecorino before serving. The recommended wine with this dish is Ischia Bianco.